J. D. SALINGER

Literature and Life: American Writers

Selected list of titles in the series:

Complete list of titles in the series available from the publisher on request

J. D. SALINGER

James Lundquist

A Frederick Ungar Book
CONTINUUM • NEW YORK

1988

The Continuum Publishing Company
370 Lexington Avenue
New York, NY 10017

Fifth Printing

Design by Anita Duncan

Printed in the United States of America

Library of Congress Cataloging in Publication Data
Lundquist, James.

  J. D. Salinger.

  (Modern literature monographs)
  Bibliography: p.
  Includes index.
  1. Salinger, Jerome David, 1919–   —Criticism and
interpretation.
PS3537 .A426Z73   813'.5'4   78–4301
ISBN 0–8044–2560–4
ISBN 0–8044–6452–9 (pbk.)

Contents

Chronology

1919   Jerome David Salinger is born 1 January 1919 in New York City to Sol and Miriam Jillich Salinger.

1930   Voted "most popular actor" at Camp Wigwam, Harrison, Maine.

1932   Parents enroll him in McBurney School, Manhattan.

1934   Sent to Valley Forge Military Academy, Pennsylvania.

1935   Becomes literary editor of Academy yearbook.

1936   Graduates from Valley Forge Military Academy.

1937   Enrolls for summer session at New York University. Goes to Austria and Poland for brief try as an apprentice in his father's import meat business.

1938   Attends Ursinus College, Collegetown, Pennsylvania, for half a semester. Writes column, "The Skipped Diploma," for *Ursinus Weekly*.

1939   Signs up for Whit Burnett's course in short-story writing at Columbia University.

1940   Publishes first story, "The Young Folks," in Burnett's *Story* (March-April issue). Another early story, "Go See Eddie," appears in the *University of Kansas City Review* (December issue).

1941   Publishes stories in *Collier's* and *Esquire*. Story about Holden Caulfield, "Slight Rebellion Off Madison," bought by *The New Yorker* but not published until 1946.

1942   Additional stories in *Collier's* and *Story*. Drafted into the U. S. Army and attends Officers, First

Sergeants, and Instructors School of the Signal Corps.

1943 Attains rank of staff sergeant and is stationed in Nashville, Tennessee. Applies for Officers' Candidate School and is transferred to the Army Counter-Intelligence Corps. Publishes story in *The Saturday Evening Post*, "The Varioni Brothers" (17 July).

1944 In Tiverton, Devonshire, England, for counter-intelligence training. Three more stories in *The Saturday Evening Post*. Lands with 4th Army Division at Utah Beach in the D-Day invasion of Normandy. Involved in five campaigns as Security Agent for the 12th Infantry Regiment.

1945 First published story about Holden Caulfield, "I'm Crazy," appears in *Collier's* (22 December). Other pieces in *Esquire*, *Story*, and *The Saturday Evening Post*.

1946 Temporary hospitalization in Nürnberg. Writes letter of adulation to Ernest Hemingway, whom he had met in France. Ninety-page novella about Holden Caulfield withdrawn by Salinger before publication. "Slight Rebellion Off Madison" finally published by *The New Yorker* (21 December).

1947 Back in the United States, publishes in *Mademoiselle* and *Cosmopolitan*.

1948 Signs contract with *The New Yorker*. "A Perfect Day for Bananafish" published in 31 January issue.

1949 "The Laughing Man" appears in *The New Yorker* (19 March) and "Down at the Dinghy" in *Harper's* (April). Moves (probably) to Westport, Connecticut, some time this year.

1950 *My Foolish Heart*, movie loosely based on "Uncle Wiggily in Connecticut," starring Susan Hayward and Dana Andrews, premieres 21 January. "For Esmé—with Love and Squalor," in *The New Yorker* (8 April), is later selected by Martha Foley as one of the distinguished short stories published in American magazines in 1950.

1951   *The Catcher in the Rye* is published by Little, Brown and Co., 16 July. Salinger avoids publicity by traveling to Europe.

1952   Travels to Mexico. Valley Forge Military Academy selects Salinger for one of three Distinguished Alumni of the Year awards.

1953   Buys ninety acres in the town of Cornish, New Hampshire. *Nine Stories* published by Little, Brown and Co., 6 April. Interviewed by Shirlie Blaney for the Windsor (Vermont) High School page that appeared monthly in the nearby Claremont (New Hampshire) *Daily Eagle.* Salinger offended when interview is printed on *Daily Eagle* editorial page, 13 November.

1955   Marriage to Claire Douglas, 17 February. "Franny" published in *The New Yorker* (29 January) and "Raise High the Roof Beam, Carpenters," also in *The New Yorker* (19 November). Daughter, Margaret Ann, born 10 December.

1957   "Zooey" published in *The New Yorker* (4 May).

1959   "Seymour: An Introduction" is published in *The New Yorker* (6 June).

1960   Son, Matthew, born 13 February.

1961   *Franny and Zooey* published by Little, Brown and Co., 14 September.

1963   *Raise High the Roof Beam, Carpenters; and Seymour: An Introduction* published by Little, Brown and Co., 28 January.

1965   "Hapworth 16, 1924," most recent published story, appears in *The New Yorker* (19 June).

I

The American Brainscape
and The Disappearing Man

This is 1979, and it has been twenty-eight years since Holden Caulfield dragged his deer-hunting cap and his prep-school heart through Manhattan. But J. D. Salinger's ideas on the true and the false in American culture, his religious solutions to the crises of alienation and isolation, and his overriding sentimentality may have had more impact on the American brainscape than anyone yet has taken into account. Since the publication of a long story, "Hapworth 16, 1924," in *The New Yorker* in 1965, Salinger has maintained a silence that has turned him into the Howard Hughes of American literature. But Salinger's lasting significance has not declined. The startling thing for many of us to realize is that the confidential ravings of Holden Caulfield, the enigma of Seymour Glass's suicide, and the pathetic pragmatism of the Jesus Prayer embraced by Franny Glass, remain part of our consciousness— and it is not just simply nostalgia for that time in the 1950s and early 1960s when Salinger's characters provided just about the only voices that did not sound phony. As a whole new generation of readers indicates, the appeal of his work is enduring. His influence remains, and we cannot get around it, perhaps cannot get over it.

We also cannot know much about Salinger the man—he is not only a recluse, he has deliberately dis-

1

appeared. But we can know something about his voice, his vision, if we read his fiction as a developing interior monologue. What emerges as we discover Salinger as the ventriloquist behind his stories is an artistry that is ever more complex and increasingly post-modern. His work from the start may be seen as a progression toward an enlightenment that is artistically as well as religiously justified. Salinger deserves to be taken seriously and in a critical way it was perhaps not possible to do when every college freshman was forced to shell out fifty cents for *The Catcher in the Rye* in English 101 and when Salinger's fiction was subject to the kind of academic overkill that was once known as "the Salinger industry."

Looking back, one can now discern at least four phases in Salinger's career. His early stories generally portray characters who feel estranged and marooned because of World War II. His second phase is represented by *The Catcher in the Rye*, and Salinger's attempt in that book to deal with estrangement and isolation through a Zen-inspired awakening and lonely benevolence. The third phase, seen in *Nine Stories*, involves bringing together the principles of Zen art and the tradition of the short story. The fourth phase is one in which Salinger's work becomes more and more experimental, resulting in the philosophical mood of his last two books, *Franny and Zooey* and *Raise High the Roof Beam, Carpenters*; and *Seymour: An Introduction*. These four phases indicate that Salinger should be read as a writer who is seeking solutions, as a writer who is trying to give direction to his thought based on an initial disturbing event. And that event is World War II.

This is not to say that Salinger should be considered a war novelist in at all the same way that one has to think about Mailer or James Jones. Nor is Salinger's relationship to the war at all as direct as that of Kurt

Vonnegut, whose life and thought, as Vonnegut has admitted himself many times, revolves around the fire-bombing of Dresden. Unlike Vonnegut, Salinger apparently did not go through a single, harrowing experience that stayed with him from that point on. Rather it was a mood that seemed to have influenced him, a mood of loneliness, isolation, ineffectuality, and a sense of being a misfit in an unfit society. This can be seen in his second published story, "The Hang of It" (*Colliers*, 12 July 1941), which deals in part with a young soldier who marches out of step with the rest of his battalion. The story is a set of strung-together scenes about an army sergeant in World War I trying to deal with an inept private who later turns out to be the commander of the regiment in which the sergeant is still trying, years later, to deal with the commander's son. But the emphasis is on the misfit hero, and the story turns on a theme that comes up again and again in Salinger—that things are not what they seem.

Many of Salinger's early stories do not deal directly with the war (and "The Hang of It" was written before he was drafted into the army) but a war atmosphere permeates them—and it is not one of patriotism, nor is it representative of the kind of thought found in so much writing to come out of the war (*The Naked and the Dead, The Young Lions, Battle Cry*) that suggests war might be hell, but at least it can make a man out of you. Instead, there is a quiet mood, one almost of despair. It is not so simple a feeling as that all gods are dead, that western civilization is "an old bitch gone in the teeth," or that the gloomy predictions of Oswald Spengler are being made fact by Hitler. Instead, there is a sense that whatever the ideological banner, the state inevitably becomes omnivorous and omnipotent and the individual is helpless against it. The question, unstated, but there nonetheless in Salinger's earliest work, is this: What can one think and do when all possible beliefs are gone?

It has been said that the survivors of World War I could be *disenchanted*, but those of World War II had to be something else because they never were *enchanted* in the first place. The title of Roland Stromberg's history of western intellectual history since 1945, *After Everything*, suggests the predicament Salinger and other writers of his generation faced. The holocaust of World War II literally left them with a sense of "after everything," asking where they could go from here when it seemed as if there were no longer any answers to the Big Questions of life. The turn was generally away from ideologies, and the feeling was one of numbness and the exhaustion of beliefs. If there was anything left, it seemed to be existentialism, with its desperate counterassertion of the life-force discovered through absurdly affirming a will to live in the face of all horrors and failures. But Salinger's reaction is both quieter and more positive, because he begins with a basic predicament—that of the misfit hero who is also a moral hero—and moves steadily toward pronouncements that assert human dignity, emphasize the importance of kindness, and suggest the possibilities for individual redemption even "after everything."

Salinger has been charged, because of his essential optimism, because of his refusal to be as grimly existential as Sartre or as bleak as Beckett (if Salinger had written *Waiting for Godot*, Godot—or at least a near relative—would have shown up to drink milk in the kitchen), of retreating into mysticism. Yet in reality, the movement of his stories suggests a kind of pilgrim's progress, a journey from the melancholia of the war stories, through the trauma of *The Catcher in the Rye* and *Nine Stories*, to the moments of revelation in the later dialogues. Again and again he writes on the relationship of man to God—or, to state it more subtly and accurately, man's relationship to the *lack* of

God and how that sense of emptiness may be treated and perhaps alleviated. At the same time, Salinger's humor, often wry, often understated, but never bitter, is there. As Albert Fowler has pointed out, "the distinctive mark of Salinger's humor is its ability to intensify the heartbreak and the horror, to bring out the catch in the throat that accompanies all the laughs. It is important . . . not that he has a saving sense of the comical but that he uses it to point up the tragic, to make his hero's plight more poignant."[1] But ultimately the humor directs us away from the tragic and toward the comic; poignancy turns into hopefulness, and the objective is enlightenment, not despair.

J. D. Salinger is an autobiographical writer. The enlightenment that is at the end of the road in his fiction is, undoubtedly, also his own. But of Salinger's life itself, not a great deal can be said because not much is known. He has chosen to preserve his privacy, and short of calling out the New Hampshire State Police, invading his compound in the town of Cornish, and injecting him with sodium pentothal, there is not a whole lot we can do about his unwillingness to tell us much about who he is and where he came from. In fact, Salinger has gone out of his way to spread rumors about himself that are not true. Information was leaked from somewhere, for example, that he was married briefly to a German physician in the 1940s. No definite evidence for this brief and supposedly unfortunate marriage has ever turned up. Another example of Salinger's distribution of information about himself is on the jacket blurb of *Franny and Zooey*, in which he writes that "I live in Westport with my dog." We do not know about the dog, but he was not living in Westport at the time. The result of this misinformation is that all sorts of wild speculation about Salinger have developed. Salinger was seen at a New York

Giants football game. Salinger was seen in Normandy, inspecting Omaha Beach, where he landed during the D-Day invasion in 1944. Salinger, in disguise, has been seen visiting various prisons. (He is supposed to have a penchant for carrying on long and sympathetic correspondences with murderers, burglars, and marijuana smugglers.) The quality of most of these rumors is suggested directly enough by Buddy Glass, Salinger's alter-ego narrator in *Seymour: An Introduction,* when he refers to "poignant get-well notes from old readers of mine who have somewhere picked up the bogus information that I spend six months of the year in a Buddhist monastery and the other six in a mental institution" (p. 153).[2]

Since the early 1950s, Salinger has lived on a ninety-acre hillside tract overlooking the Connecticut River. And that, apparently, is pretty much where he has remained ever since, stories of disguised appearances and bizarre pseudonyms on motel registers to the contrary. And what is known of his life before and after his move to New Hampshire may be summarized briefly in relationship to his early writing.

Jerome David Salinger was born in New York City on New Year's Day, 1919, to a Jewish father and a Christian mother. His father, Sol, was an importer of hams and cheeses—and eventually a very prosperous man. Salinger was reportedly solemn and quiet as a child. He had no brothers and only one sister, Doris, eight years older. Salinger attended public schools in Manhattan's upper west side and was nothing like the Wise Child he makes the Glass family children out to be in the legend he builds around them. His grades were only slightly above average, and arithmetic apparently stumped him altogether. Someone has found out that his IQ test score was an average 104 and that his behavior in school was occasionally bad.[3] A different view of Salinger as a boy comes out of the impression he made at Camp Wigwam in Harrison, Maine, where he went when he was eleven. That summer he is supposed to have turned into a good tennis player and—let's not place too much significance in this—was voted "most popular actor."

When he was thirteen, Salinger's parents enrolled him in Manhattan's "highly rated" McBurney School out of concern for his studies. He flunked out a year later, but we get a trace of the Salinger insouciance in his statement at the enrollment interview that he was interested in dramatics and tropical fish. We get an impression of Salinger in adolescence from a friend who recalled of him at this time that "he wanted to do unconventional things. For hours, no one in the family knew where he was or what he was doing; he just showed up for meals. He was a nice boy, but he was the kind of kid who, if you wanted to have a card game, wouldn't join in."[4]

The next step for a boy in Salinger's social position, with his problems at the age of fifteen, was inevitable—he was sent to Valley Forge Military Academy in the Pennsylvania Hills. It is here that certain biographical facts begin to build in accounting for Salinger as a writer. Perhaps it was at Valley Forge that Salinger developed a sense of being a misfit, of having been sent away to become part of an alien institution, and that what is needed, what is missed, is a larger, closer family. But that might be pushing Salinger's development as the writer he turned out to be a little too far back. At any rate, Valley Forge is the model for Pencey Prep in *The Catcher in the Rye*, and like Holden, Salinger managed the fencing team. Other related facts that have been dug up include the information that one of Salinger's fellow cadets did jump from a window, like James Castle in *Catcher*, and that another cadet, somewhat like Holden, was expelled and ended up in a west-coast mental institution. But

Salinger was not Holden Caulfield. One of his classmates at Valley Forge, Alton McCloskey, a retired
milk dealer in Lock Haven, Pennsylvania, did remember going along with Salinger to hit the local beer taps
after lights out at the academy, but McCloskey could
not remember Salinger dropping out the way Holden
does, and did not rate Salinger as much of a nonconformist. He was so little a nonconformist, indeed, that
as literary editor of *Crossed Sabres*, the school yearbook, he wrote a poetic tribute to the school that is
still sung at Last Parade. (It should be pointed out,
however, that even though Salinger is listed as the
author of the lyrics in the Valley Forge yearbook,
there is some typically mysterious uncertainty about
whether he actually wrote them.)

Salinger did do some other writing at Valley
Forge, and before his graduation in June 1936, he had
written his first stories. That he was interested in writing while at the academy is apparent, but his com-
mitment to a literary career seemed anything but
great. He tried a few weeks of classes at New York
University during the summer session in 1937 and then
set off for Vienna with his father to become a busi-
nessman. "I was supposed to apprentice myself to the
Polish ham business," Salinger wrote in 1944. "They
finally dragged me off to Bydgoszcz for a couple of
months, where I slaughtered pigs, wagoned through
the snow with the big slaughter-master. Came back to
America and tried college for half a semester, but quit
like a quitter."[5]

What was Salinger to do next? He seemed to have
no future, he was unsuited for business, and his academic problems made a professional career unlikely.
So he did what many others did during the great
depression—he enrolled in a short-story writing class.
Jobs may have been in short supply at the time and

money was tight, but there was a booming market for the short story. People were spending what little money they had on cheap entertainment, and magazines were one form of that. There was enough demand for short fiction that a reasonably talented writer could realistically expect to sell at least a few stories somewhere.

The course Salinger enrolled in was Whit Burnett's famous writing class at Columbia University. The course was famous because Burnett, along with his wife Hallie, was editor of *Story* magazine, which published fiction of the sort not looked for by the slick magazines. *Story*, for example, printed the early work of Tennessee Williams, Mailer, Truman Capote, and others.

The influence of Burnett on Salinger is something that can be overemphasized, but whether Salinger learned anything directly from Burnett or not, his first published story, "The Young Folks," came out in the March-April, 1940, issue of the magazine. The story is greatly weakened by inept dialogue and description (two problems Salinger never quite overcomes), but it introduces one of Salinger's most lasting themes: "Raw adolescence exposed to the deceitful ploys of the adult world."[6] The story centers on a young man at a teenage party who is falsely accused by an equally pathetic young woman of propositioning her. The hero, Jameson, is one of Salinger's innocents, and the girl is a phony. Yes, it is easy to see Holden Caulfield in Jameson, because the basic predicament, one that is used again and again by Salinger, "is that of a moral hero forced to compromise his integrity with a pragmatic society. What disaffiliates the hero is his peculiar off-center vision which sensitizes and distorts his sense of truth in a false world."[7] And off-center vision, oversensitization, a distorted sense of truth, all complicated by a false world, this is what Jameson and so many other Salinger characters have to face as they come to realize that things are not what they seem.

As Arthur Mizener has pointed out, Salinger's early stories are important not because of their quality (they read as what they are—the attempts of a young writer to apply, usually mechanically, the "techniques" that were emphasized in the then-popular short-story writing courses), but because "They show us Salinger's preoccupation with close personal relations, particularly family relations. They make clear his marked preference for first-person narration and interior monologue. And they show the related difficulty he has in saying what he wants to and at the same time constructing a 'well-made' plot."[8] Some of these preoccupations are apparent in "The Hang of It," and in a slight satirical piece, "The Heart of a Broken Story," that appeared in the September 1941 *Esquire*, but they are strikingly present in the fourth of his pieces, "The Long Debut of Lois Taggert," which was published in the September-October, 1942, *Story*.

"The Long Debut of Lois Taggett" also introduces Salinger's strange and sometimes obsessive use of "signs" in setting forth personal relationships; that is, the stories often begin and often turn on bizarre personal gestures and oddly distracting objects. Lois, a society girl, has her first marriage end after her husband puts out a cigarette in her hand and hits her foot with a golf club. She marries again, this time to Carl Curfman, who is a gentle and admirable person except for one problem—he insists that he has to wear white socks; colored ones hurt his feet. What else can a girl like Lois do? She abuses Carl, taunts him, and makes him miserable. All this changes, however, when her baby smothers while sleeping, and at this point the story collapses. Instead of becoming worse, as the reader fully expects Lois to do, she reverses herself and becomes an admirable person—even to the point of letting Carl wear his white socks again. The change is sudden and inexplicable, and this is a difficulty with many of Salinger's stories, a difficulty that perhaps arises because of his insistence that his heroes and heroines move toward a maturing kind of moral awareness.

With his next story, "Personal Notes on an Infantryman" (*Colliers*, 12 December 1942), Salinger returns to the concern with World War II and the crisis atmosphere it has generated that remains with him throughout much of his writing in the 1940s. James E. Miller is certainly correct in pointing out that "if we are allowed to read any autobiography at all in his work, we may readily guess that the war was responsible for, or at least brought to the surface, an alienation from modern existence so profound as to manifest itself at times in an overpowering spiritual nausea."[9] "Personal Notes of an Infantryman" is a story in which alienation and spiritual nausea figure, although it is a contrived narrative in which a defense plant foreman volunteers for army duty when he learns that one of his sons has been wounded in action. The recruiting officer, who tells the story, turns out to be the man's other son. The narrator, who feels guilty about his stateside military job, worries about how to tell his mother what has happened, and he wants to avoid using "phony" language—the first time the word that Salinger was later to make famous in *The Catcher in the Rye* appears in his work.

Several other aspects of Salinger's developing method appear in this story as well. One is the use of what Mizener calls "suspended explanation"—"we are frequently astonished and delighted when we catch our first glimpse of the precise connections between what had before seemed unconnected events."[10] In this case the words *astonished* and *delighted* are a little strong, but there is some surprise in finding out what the relationship between the recruiting officer and the older man he is talking to actually is. Another Salinger characteristic, as Warren French in his important book length study of Salinger explains, is that the narrator is the first of Salinger's "evaders." The narrator cannot look his father in the eyes. Salinger's characters often talk indirectly, from behind shower curtains and over telephones; many of them are so filled with guilt and anxiety that they are unable to look directly at others and talk.[11]

Guilt, anxiety, and evasiveness figure prominently in "The Varioni Brothers," the first of Salinger's stories to appear in *The Saturday Evening Post* (17 July 1943). This story represents a temporary departure from Salinger's war-consciousness; but it does hint at his growing concern with the serious development of his own writing in the way it centers on the role of the artist and the theme of art versus money. The story deals with two brothers. Joe is a college English teacher and a talented fiction writer. Sonny is a composer of popular songs. Sonny encourages Joe to give up the novel he is working on and to concentrate on making money by writing lyrics for Sonny's tunes. Joe gives in, and soon Sonny's prediction comes true; the money starts piling up. Sonny, however, gets involved with gamblers, who kill Joe, mistaking him for his brother. Years later, Sonny, consumed by guilt, picks up Joe's novel and, at last appreciating Joe's genius, tries to finish writing it. The significance of the story is that by now Salinger had sold six stories; he had quickly established himself as a professional writer—but would he sell out like Joe? The business of the unfinished novel also points to something else: Salinger's uncertainty from the start about whether he could be a novelist. Several times he has stated that the short story is his most comfortable form. *The*

Catcher in the Rye is the only one of his books that could actually be classified as a novel, and even with it there is a problem: It does read as if it started out as a story and was simply expanded.

But we have no indication that Salinger was even working on a novel at this time. In 1942 he had been drafted into the Army and attended the Officers, First Sergeants, and Instructors School of the Signal Corps. In 1943, continuing to write as often as he could, often spending weekend passes in hotel rooms with his typewriter, he was stationed in Nashville, Tennessee, with the rank of Staff Sergeant. He applied for Officers' Candidate School and was transferred to the Army Counter-Intelligence Corps. He was sent to Tiverton, Devonshire, in England for his Counter-Intelligence training (Tiverton is apparently the setting for one of the most impressive stories in *Nine Stories*, "For Esmé—With Love and Squalor").

Salinger has never commented at length on his wartime experiences, but even in outline it is possible to sense what degree of influence they may have had on him. Like Vonnegut, Salinger participated in the D-Day invasion of Normandy. Just five hours after the first assault forces hit Utah Beach on June 6, 1944, Salinger landed with the 4th Infantry Division. His job was the sort of thing Salinger himself might have invented. He worked alone, and his assignment was to discover Gestapo agents through interrogating French civilians and captured Germans. The indirectness in his stories, the suspended explanations, the kind of veiled questioning that one character directs at another—all of this fits Salinger's role as a counter-intelligence officer. Secrecy, surprise, and sudden insight into squalor and private heroism as well as private betrayal are what Salinger had to deal with in his wartime assignment as well as in his fiction.

In France, Salinger sought out Ernest Hemingway, who was spending his days as a part-time war correspondent and full-time adventurer. Salinger found Hemingway to be friendly and generous and not at all as hard and tough as his writing suggested. They got along well together, and Hemingway offered to look at Salinger's work.[12] In a possibly apocryphal account, Hemingway was reportedly so pleased with Salinger's work ("Jesus, he has a helluva talent," Hemingway is supposed to have said) that he pulled out his Luger and blasted the head off a chicken.[13] Hemingway's biographer, Carlos Baker, came across a letter from Salinger to Hemingway, written 27 July 1946, in which Salinger facetiously explains his temporary hospitalization in Nürnberg as the result of an attempt to find a nurse who resembled the Catherine Barkley of Hemingway's *A Farewell to Arms.* Salinger goes on to say that he was continuing to write as often as he could and that he was working on a play about a boy named Holden Caulfield and his sister Phoebe. Salinger told Hemingway that he had been fascinated with the stage ever since he had played the role of Raleigh in *Journey's End,* a romantic war drama by R. C. Sherwood. And, in a possibly significant statement about the autobiographical relationship between Salinger and his most famous character, Salinger indicated, according to Baker, that when the play was completed, he planned to act the part of Holden, "suitably disguised with crew-cut hair and a Max Factor belly dimple, and to persuade Margaret O'Brien to do the part of Phoebe."[14] Salinger also told Hemingway that he had finished two more of his "incestuous" short stories, but that his plans for a book had been temporarily put aside. He did recall, however, "that his talks with Ernest in Europe had given him his only hopeful minutes of the entire war, and named himself national chairman of the Hemingway Fan Clubs."[15]

If Salinger's writing was actually influenced by that of Hemingway, we have little indication of it. His admiration of Hemingway seems more like that of a younger writer for an older one who was then near the peak of his fame. But what is perhaps most important about Salinger's letter to Hemingway is his reference to his "incestuous" short stories. In his early work, Salinger often used the same character types and then, after "The Last Day of the Last Furlough" (*Saturday Evening Post*, 15 July 1944), in which he introduces Babe Gladwaller and Vincent Caulfield, Holden's older brother, he begins returning to the same characters. This tendency is to continue until, with *Nine Stories* and the invention of the Glass family, his related narratives all seem to create each other.

In some ways, Babe Gladwaller can be seen as Salinger's re-creation of himself. In "The Last Day of the Last Furlough," Babe is spending his last day at home before going overseas. He likes small children and reading (Tolstoy, Dostoevsky, and Fitzgerald), and he desperately wants to avoid hurting the feelings of others—and it is on this point that the story centers: Babe wants to conceal the truth from his mother that he is being sent overseas. One of Salinger's most tightly written early stories, "The Last Day of the Last Furlough" develops in a series of main scenes (a sure indication of his interest in playwriting at the time).

The first scene shows us Babe taking a sled and meeting his ten-year-old sister, Mattie, at school. They talk about *Wuthering Heights* in a kind of adult-child exchange that later becomes one of the main characteristics of Salinger's fiction. These encounters are always Rousseauistic in the way the child, wise as the child may seem, is presented. The child always represents the individual born good and corrupted by institutions (the school-yard is significant here). This is a major idea in Salinger and will be discussed more fully in its importance to *The Catcher in the Rye* and *Nine Stories*, but Salinger's devotion to what Leslie Fiedler terms "the cult of the child" must be understood at the start as "an example not of the innocence of the spirit but of the eye."[16] In this, the child does give us what is, symbolically at least, an unfallen way of perceiving the world. But Mattie's "unfallenness" is used ironically by Salinger to portray the implication of Babe (and us all) in the guilt she shares but about which she has not yet learned to lie.

The second scene takes place at home, where Babe's friend Vincent Caulfield, a soap opera writer in real life, is waiting for Babe and Mattie. Vincent's occupation represents another of Salinger's lasting obsessions—the writer as sell-out. This concern goes back to "The Varioni Brothers" and extends forward to Holden Caulfield's older brother, B. D., who has sold out to Hollywood, and even to Buddy Glass, who works as a "writer in residence" at a women's college. Salinger's later refusal to sell his major works to the film studios and his refusal to become a public figure are understandable enough in the consideration he gave this matter at a time when he was successfully writing popular formula fiction for slick magazines.

As the second scene develops, Vincent joins Babe and his family at dinner, where Babe's father launches into some of his World War I stories. Babe interrupts his father and argues that it is wrong to romanticize war—something that never happens in Salinger's own war stories. If anything, Salinger usually depicts war as dull and dreary, where the worst danger is loneliness and boredom for the soldier.

In another scene, Babe and Vincent go out on a double date. Babe's date is silly but he is irrationally attracted to her. This is another of Salinger's characteristics; his heroes, from Babe and his date, to Holden Caulfield and Sally Hayes, to Seymour Glass and his nail-painting wife in "A Perfect Day for Bananafish" from *Nine Stories*, tend to be fascinated with women who are foolish, contrary, and sometimes even fatal. This treatment of women does change, however, in his later writing and could simply be seen as a part of Salinger's immaturity in the 1940s. Vincent tries to point out, however, that the smart, reliable girl he is with is the kind Babe should be looking for. But Babe's very name suggests his nature—like so many of Salinger's characters, he is in love with innocence, and it is the very childishness of his date that appeals to him. Sophistication without a moral stance, which is what Vincent's date represents, is but another symptom of the societal corruption that distresses Babe.

Babe returns home in the final scene and, in a moment that looks ahead to *The Catcher in the Rye*, he goes into Mattie's room. She wakes up and makes him confess that he has indeed been ordered overseas. It is an example of the child, in her very childishness, sensing what is wrong and knowing instinctively the disturbing nature of Babe's anguish. The scene concludes with Babe's mother also finding out the truth. Like *The Catcher in the Rye*, "The Last Day of the Last Furlough" poignantly details a last attempt at hanging onto innocence and youth.

An incidental point about the story, however, is that Vincent mentions that his younger brother, Holden, has run away from school. The Holden who is mentioned does not seem to quite be a prototype for the Holden of *The Catcher in the Rye*; the earlier Holden is referred to as tough—something the later Holden certainly is not. It is clear that Salinger was at first more interested in the fictional possibilities of Vincent than he was with Holden, for in "This Sandwich Has No Mayonnaise" (*Esquire*, October 1945), a story selected by Martha Foley as one of the distinguished short stories published in American magazines in that year and later included in *Best Short Stories of 1946*, Salinger focuses on Vincent. "This Sandwich Has No Mayonnaise" is a disturbing account of Vincent's depression over what ought to be a minor incident. Vincent, now training in Georgia for the Air Corps, is responsible for loading a truck to take men to a dance. Too many men get on, however, because Vincent fouls up. What is bothering him is not that so much but the report of Holden missing in action. The emphasis on loss and on mental instability brought on by the atmosphere of the war makes this one of Salinger's most disturbing stories and brings out what is usually overlooked by those who are shocked by the suicide of Seymour in "A Perfect Day for Bananafish," that, as Mizener stresses, "there is in his work a very high incidence of emotional collapse and even violent death."[17]

But the "incestuous" nature of Salinger's fiction on the Caulfield matter is apparent in that Salinger turns away from Vincent and resurrects Holden in a different form in "I'm Crazy" (*Collier's*, 22 December 1945). Here the Holden of *The Catcher in the Rye* appears for the first time in two scenes that Salinger later expands—Holden's talk with his history teacher before he leaves for prep school, and his talk with his sister, Phoebe, in her bedroom. Holden is also featured in another story, "Slight Rebellion off Madison" (*The New Yorker*, 21 December 1946) in which we see his date with Sally Hayes, another incident that becomes part of *The Catcher in the Rye*.

In technique, however, these stories are not quite the early versions of scenes from Salinger's novel that one might at first think they are. Holden is seen here as mainly a crazy kid—not at all as complex a character as he eventually becomes. And the distinctive narrative style of *The Catcher in the Rye* is simply not there ("Slight Rebellion off Madison," for instance, is told in the third person). A further complication in understanding Salinger's conception of Holden is that the second Holden story was actually accepted by *The New Yorker* in 1941 and set into type but was then delayed because the subject matter did not seem serious or appropriate enough in the grim days after Pearl Harbor (Lucky Strike Green was not the only American institution to go to war; *The New Yorker* was another). What this means (again the incestuousness) is that Salinger most likely had Holden in mind before Vincent. Holden thus gave birth to Vincent who in turn gave birth to Holden. This is by no means an unusual process for a writer, but it indicates how Salinger began developing a repertoire of characters from the start, and it is not surprising that he eventually winds up centering on the Glass family in his last two books.

Babe Gladwaller remains in the repertoire through two sequels to "Last Day of the Last Furlough." In "A Boy in France" (*Saturday Evening Post*, 31 March 1945) Babe, in a foxhole, goes to sleep reading a letter from Mattie. Amid the horrible destruction of war, Mattie's voice comes to Babe as a comforting reminder of his and his civilization's own lost innocence. In "The Stranger" (*Collier's*, 1 December 1945), Babe has returned home and takes Mattie to visit Vincent's ex-girl friend, now Mrs. Bob Polk. Vincent has been killed in the Hurtgen Forest. As Babe tells her this, we learn that she had broken up with Vincent because of his cynicism and had gotten married before his death. The innocence of Mattie (even though Mattie's innocence is being eroded through the education she receives in accompanying Babe and listening to him) forms a contrast to the experience of the ex-girl friend. But the Babe Gladwaller stories end here. Some readers have seen in Babe a prototype for Seymour Glass. Does he become Seymour and marry the silly girl of "Last Furlough"? The conceptual transition is there. A more likely explanation for the sudden disappearance of Babe from Salinger's repertoire is that Salinger seems to have been trying to develop the same sensibilities in Babe that he later does more successfully in Holden. Babe is ultimately unworkable as a character. He is too uncomplicated for his age. He is made to act like Holden in many ways, but he is simply too old.

Salinger's output was consistent during the war years, and, given his later production, was almost what might be termed prolific as he steadily built a reputation as a writer of short stories. In "Soft-Boiled Sergeant" (*The Saturday Evening Post*, 15 April 1944) he demonstrated his mastery of the indirectly told story in one of his most moving, although sometimes maudlin, wartime pieces. The hero of the story, Sgt. Burke, is extremely concerned about others, even to the point of letting a young, homesick soldier (the narrator) wear the Sergeant's decorations on his underwear (another example of Salinger's peculiar reliance on "signs") in order to help him adjust to barracks life. Sgt. Burke is later killed rescuing frightened soldiers at Pearl Harbor. Burke is physically repulsive and the women he desires reject him, but the girl to whom the story is told cries when she finds out what has happened to him. Is she the type of girl Burke should have sought out or is she merely responding to the story as a story? Salinger is subtly raising some questions concerning the relationship between fiction, the experience on which it is based, and the reaction of the audience.

Much of his other writing during this period is not so subtle and not so convincing. "Both Parties Concerned" (*The Saturday Evening Post*, 26 February 1944) is an example, although it does concentrate on a problem that Salinger comes back to again and again —marriage. A couple has married young. They leave their baby and go out every night. The woman finally leaves because the marriage is not serious enough. The husband resolves to grow up, and he wins his wife back. The story, like the marriage it deals with, is insubstantial and unconvincing. "Once A Week Won't Kill You" (*Story*, November-December 1944) is somewhat better. Aunt Rena, in her fifties, her life shattered years earlier when a soldier left her and failed to return, centers her existence on listening to the radio and being taken to the movies once a week. She lives with her nephew, who is entering the army, and his wife. Her nephew does not want her to worry about him and tries to get his wife to promise she will take Rena to the movies once a week. She refuses to promise. In his concern for others, the nephew is a typical Salinger hero, and the wife is a type that perhaps appears too often in Salinger.

Salinger's treatment of women is not always unsympathetic or hostile in these early stories. "Elaine" (*Story*, March-April 1945) gives us another side of Salinger and a significant clue to an attitude toward sexuality that becomes increasingly apparent in his fiction. Elaine, a beautiful but mentally retarded girl, is apparently seduced by and then marries a movie usher named Teddy. Elaine's mother makes her abandon her husband, however, and the story ends with Elaine going to a nice, "safe" Henry Fonda movie. Elaine's plight is treated sympathetically by Salinger, and on the surface the message seems to be that Elaine, as well as most people, is better off going to movies than in trying to deal with complexities of life that are indeed beyond her. In this respect, we can see how Salinger tends to divide his characters between those who are capable of insight and feeling (Babe Gladwaller, Holden Caulfield, Seymour Glass) and those who are congenitally unable to respond to life except through clichés and the unreality of the movie screen (Elaine, Babe's silly girlfriend, Seymour's wife). Beneath all of this there might be something else. As Warren French suggests concerning "Elaine," this story may serve to "throw light upon critical episodes of *The Catcher in the Rye* and of *Franny and Zooey,* in both of which characters are literally sickened at the thought of sex."[18] At the very least, Salinger is suspicious of marriage as a solution to anything, and at a time when fiction was steadily becoming more sexually explicit, his in fact becomes less so.

A crucial story in understanding Salinger's attitudes toward love and marriage is "The Inverted Forest" (*Cosmopolitan,* December 1947), actually a short novel of 24,000 words, in which marital responsibility, repressed sexuality, and artistic integrity are all linked. French argues that "The Inverted Forest" is also "of major importance in understanding Salinger's artistic vision and techniques,"[19] but the incredibly fantastic and muddled plot along with uncertainty in point-of-view make such a claim seem overstated. The story is an important one, however, because it possibly gives us some insight into what Salinger was thinking about himself at the time when he was freshly out of the service and back living with his parents on Park Avenue. Gwynn and Blotner, in their book, *The Fiction of J. D. Salinger* (Pittsburgh: University of Pittsburgh Press, 1958), the first comprehensive study of Salinger's work, classify "The Inverted Forest" along with "The Varioni Brothers" as the "Destroyed Artist Melodramas," which show "Salinger struggling with a theme he wants to be able to handle but which he really does not seem to understand."[20] He does not understand it, as the structures of the stories indicate, because the theme is too close to him. In a painfully obvious way, we see first the danger of money in the artist's life in the "sell out" of Joe Varioni. And then we see the danger of sex and marriage in "The Inverted Forest"—a danger that triggers near-phobic reactions, and if one chooses to take it as something approaching a biographical statement, it presents a disturbing picture of Salinger and his own anxieties concerning his future.

The story opens in 1918 when Corinne von Nord-hoffen, eleven years old and the daughter of a German baron and an heiress who committed suicide (again, it is important to note how often suicide or suicidal tendencies figure in Salinger's writing), is having a birthday party on Long Island. Corinne is distressed because Raymond Ford, a poor boy who is her favorite is not there. She goes looking for him only to see him being taken away by his hard-bitten waitress mother in one of her many and sudden moves. Corinne's father dies, she goes to Wellesley, and then spends three years in Europe, her only love in all this time being a boy who is killed when he falls from the running board of her car. After she returns to New York, the narrator of the story, Robert Waner, an old college friend who once loved her, gets her a job on a news magazine, and she eventually becomes a drama critic. When she turns thirty, Waner gives her a book of poems by—who else?—Ray Ford, who has become a well-known poet and who also is an instructor at Columbia. She is especially taken with the lines that give the story its title, "Not wasteland, but a great inverted forest/with all foliage underground." She seeks Ray out and learns what happened to him since they were separated as children. Because of the example of his alcoholic mother, he has never taken a drink, never smoked, and he has been unable to love. He had worked at a Florida racetrack until an older woman rescued him, became his patroness, and let him educate himself in her library. After ten weeks of dates and confessions, Corinne and Ray get married despite the gloomy warning of Waner that Ray is a hopeless psychotic and that he cannot love her.

Soon after the honeymoon, Bunny Croft, a college girl with literary aspirations, begins to appeal to Ray. At this point, the narration shifts from Waner's hands, and in an unlikely note from Corinne, we suddenly discover that the rest of the story is going to be in the form of a private detective's notebook. Before long, Corinne is drinking heavily, Ray is drinking heavily, and the marriage falls apart. Ray and Bunny leave New York together, and Corinne is counselled by Howie Croft, Bunny's husband of ten years, who has seen just how shallow, drunken, and adulterous Bunny is. A year-and-a-half later, Corinne tracks Ray and Bunny to a midwestern slum. They are both down-and-out alcoholics, Ray trying to arrange papers on a card table and Bunny trying to write her twelfth pathetic and unpublishable book. In a drunken speech, Ray tells Corinne that for him there is no escape. He suggests that his crude mother finally has passed her alcoholism on to him and that Bunny, alcoholic like his mother and strangely associated with her in his mind, has got him for good.

The idea of inversion runs throughout the story. Ray is the artist, the one with the inverted forest, in that the beauty he sees, the beauty which leads to his art, is all underground. His roots, his background, are exposed and there for someone like Corinne to see as she finds out about his mother and his education, but the real world of the artist is something only he can see. Corinne tries to get into that world, and so does Bunny, and, somehow, it is destroyed. The foliage wilts, and all Ray has left is the wasteland—the cruel world that has made him what it is. The story is confused in its allegorical implications, and the reader tends to feel more sorry for Corinne than for Ray, but the sheer threat of sexuality and marriage is an inescapable presence.

When a writer like Salinger who is reticent about

his own biography writes a story such as "The Inverted Forest," he opens himself up to psychological
speculation of what is often the worst kind. And a
danger in reading Salinger is to make too much of
such stories. One thing is apparent, however, and it is
what many readers and critics have long pointed out,
that sex generally has a destructive effect in Salinger's
stories. We should realize, though, that Salinger is
from the start an extremely moral writer, and sexual
morality is no small part of his moral vision. Salinger is
concerned with how people treat one another and
whether it is possible for them to deal with one another in kindness. For many of his characters, love is
simply impossible, or is presented in impossible terms,
and this is what makes sex so negative a factor in his
work. Ray is a psychotic—he cannot love Corinne, and
if he tries to, he will destroy his art, which has its basis
in his psychosis. How much of Salinger himself is in
this? Draw your own conclusion.

Whatever biographical elements it contains, the
kind of veiled introspection concerning the role of the
writer and the threats to his artistry that we can discern in "The Inverted Forest" does indicate a shift in
Salinger's work away from the kind of formula writing
required by *The Saturday Evening Post, Collier's,* and
Cosmopolitan. Salinger was spending his nights in
Greenwich Village arguing with friends, artists, and
other young writers, and he developed a reputation
that would soon become out of character, a reputation
involving the number of girls he would bring with him
to the Village. He reportedly met most of these girls in
the drugstore of the Barbizon Hotel for Women in
Manhattan, and his friends recalled that he was interested in them at least partly because of the dialogue
he was storing up. Even at that, he was reticent about
himself. An old anecdote has it that one girl returned
to the Hotel Barbizon believing she had been out with

the goalie for the Montreal Canadiens. But some of his other dates remembered something else, that he was eager to give them reading lists on Zen Buddhism (a topic that will be explored in its relationship to *The Catcher in the Rye, Nine Stories,* and the later books, but a topic that cannot be underestimated in its influence on Salinger's thinking and his sudden maturation as a writer).

This maturation is signalled in another way as well—his signing of a *New Yorker* contract with the publication of "A Perfect Day for Bananafish" in the 31 January 1948 issue. All but two of the stories later collected in *Nine Stories* were published in *The New Yorker,* and Salinger soon became known as a "*New Yorker* writer." For the first time, he was writing with consistent editorial advice, and he was forced by the "*New Yorker* style" to correct the kind of narrative sprawl he drifted into with "The Inverted Forest." City wit, surface brilliance, and stylized irony of situation is what mention of *The New Yorker* would bring to mind in the 1940s. But the style meant more than that. The typical story published by the magazine had no more than two or three characters, the essential situation a moment of crisis in the life of one of the characters. The relationships leading up to the moment are only suggested through the tone of the dialogues and gestures (an important moment in any good Salinger story). The plot is underplayed and narrative is minimized (plot and narrative are among Salinger's weak points from the start). The reader oddly remains unidentified with the problems and remains on the outside, but is made aware that the crisis is "a generic one of our time and place."[21] That Salinger took all of this to heart is apparent in the remark by Alfred Kazin that Salinger "obviously writes to and for some particular editorial mind he identifies with *The New Yorker;* look up the stories he used to write for *The Saturday Evening Post* and *Cosmopolitan,* and you will see that just as married people get to look alike by reproducing each other's facial expressions, so a story by Salinger and a passage of commentary in *The New Yorker* now tend to resemble each other."[22]

As his writing became more serious, Salinger began the series of withdrawals that would eventually take him to his compound in Cornish. He first moved to a cottage in Tarrytown, New York, trying to keep his address as secret as possible—a plan that apparently did not work, since he was forced to hide out in a room near the Third Avenue El to finish *The Catcher in the Rye*. He escaped some of the publicity following the success of the novel, when it was published in 1951, by going to Europe. The next year he visited Mexico, and in 1953 he bought his ninety acres in New Hampshire. One of the legends that sprang up at this time is that he liked to hike across the river in the wintertime to Windsor, Vermont, and spend his time kidding the teenagers in a local hangout. This legend has some substance because the only reporter whose questions he has ever answered was a sixteen-year-old Windsor high school girl who wrote an article on him for the Claremont, New Hampshire, *Daily Eagle* (13 November 1953).

The girl, Shirlie Blaney, remembers that Salinger was not entirely a recluse when he first moved to Cornish. He went to cocktail parties with local teachers and military officers, and entertained them in turn. He also went to basketball and football games at Windsor High School, and Shirlie and other teenage friends would drive out to see him. The first time she went along on one of these visits, Shirlie recalls, he cried, "Come on in!" Then he brought out Cokes and potato chips and began playing records. Everytime they tried to leave, he would say, "Stick around. I'll play another record."[23]

"He was just like one of the gang," Shirlie said in a 1961 conversation with Ernest Haveman of *Life* magazine, "except that he never did anything silly the way the rest of us did. He always knew who was going with whom, and if anybody was having trouble at school, and we all looked up to him, especially the renegades. He'd play whatever record we asked for on his hi-fi—my favorite was *Swan Lake*—and when we started to leave, he'd always want to play just one more."[24] Some of his quests began to suspect that he was writing another book about teenagers and that they were being used as his guinea pigs. And not all of their parents were pleased with whatever the relationship between Salinger and his young friends might have been. "I'd sit there and wonder, why is he doing this?" Shirlie confessed.

The interview came about this way. Windsor High School had a monthly page that served as the school paper in the *Daily Eagle* of nearby Claremont. One of the problems was finding enough news at Windsor High to fill even the limited space they had. One afternoon as Shirlie and other staff members of the monthly page were trying to come up with some copy, Shirlie looked out the window and saw Salinger —the students called him Jerry—on the street. She ran outside, explained that she would like to write a story about him for the school paper, and wanted to know if she could ask him a few questions. He drew back suspiciously and then, because it was only to be for the student page, he agreed. They went into Harrington's Spa and he told Shirlie a few things about his life and work habits. Neither the interview nor the resulting article was very thorough, and Salinger probably threw in several of his notorious fabrications—among them that he once worked as an entertainer on the liner *Kungsholm*.

Salinger looked for the results of the interview in the next issue of the high-school page; and when he did not see it, he called Shirlie to find out what had happened, since he had agreed to answer questions on the assumption that the story would appear only in the student section of the paper. A few days later, the article was printed under the headline, "An Interview with an Author," on—to the horror of Salinger—the editorial page. That was the last conversation Shirlie or any of the other Windsor teenagers had with Salinger. The next time they went to see him, he refused to answer the door.[25]

But some knowledge of Salinger's writing habits in Cornish did come out of this, and other inquiries, that inquisitive—and usually disappointed—reporters have made. Salinger's house sits back from his mailbox behind a high woven-wood fence, a mile from the nearest paved road. He does his writing in a concrete-block studio, which is set downhill from the house and has a fireplace, two windows, and a plastic roof that serves as a skylight. On the walls are cup hooks upon which he hangs clipboards full of notes. He has been known to work as long as fifteen hours a day, throwing much of his work away (*The Catcher in the Rye* was once, according to various reports, anywhere from four-to-ten times as long as the published version). Salinger wants no interruptions when he is working, and if anyone tries to reach him in the bunker by phone, "the house had damned well be burning down," a relative has said.[26]

At times he has been seen working in the nearby Dartmouth library or eating at a Howard Johnson's in the area—but not very often, and sometimes not for years.

As John Skow has suggested, Salinger's withdrawal may partly be explained by pointing out that his social needs are met by his family. At a party in Manchester, Vermont, in 1953, Salinger met an English-born Radcliffe student named Claire Douglas, who later visited the thirty-four-year-old writer several times in Cornish. She soothed her family's worries about her relationship with Salinger by telling them that he lived "with his mother, sister, fifteen Buddhist monks, and a yogi who stood on his head."[27] But Claire abruptly dropped Salinger and married a young man from the Harvard Business School. Just as suddenly, she ended the marriage within a year and returned to Cornish, where she and Salinger were married in 1955. Salinger's wedding present was supposedly the story "Franny." Like the heroine of the story, Claire had once been hung up on the "Jesus prayer," and Franny also has "Claire's looks, mannerisms, and—the sort of private salute that amuses the author—Claire's blue suitcase."[28] Salinger gave a wedding party attended by his mother, his sister (then a dress-buyer at Bloomingdale's in New York), and Claire's ex-husband. But Salinger was not pleased with the wedding present he received from the people of Cornish. Pranksters at the town meeting elected him Town Hargreave—an honorary office customarily awarded to the most recently married man, whose duties consist of rounding up runaway pigs.

Salinger has continued to live his quiet life at Cornish with Claire and their two children (Margaret Ann, born 10 December 1955, and Matthew, born on 13 February 1960). And what is he working on? There has been much speculation, most of it centering on the possibility of a Glass-family trilogy. And Skow may be right in guessing that, "Since his marriage, the author has exhausted himself, and his supply of sociability, in a protracted effort to give his legend structure and direction, to deal with characters who speak his own most shadowed thoughts, and to solve the snarls

caused by piecemeal publication. His face, after . . .
years of struggle, shows the pain of an artistic battle
whose outcome still cannot be seen."[29]

Salinger's appeal to readers in the 1950s was
partly a matter of his inscrutability, not only in his life,
but in his writing as well. Circular arguments were
carried on over whether or not Teddy was murdered
by his sister, whether or not Franny was pregnant, or
whether or not Holden Caulfield is insane at the end
of the novel or if he has somehow been redeemed.
Salinger remains inscrutable still, and this quality perhaps now angers readers more than it pleases them. To
be certain, his long silence as a writer and his insistence on personal privacy makes him a difficult writer
to understand and to read with much sympathy. After
all, most of us at least like to know who it is we are
reading. And it is easy to be so driven by frustration
that we agree with French's outrageous but altogether
reasonable suggestion that Salinger's behavior "may
actually result from an inability to make the social
adjustments expected of mature members of society."[30] However, it may be better for us to pay some
attention to one of Salinger's few comments on his
unwillingness to be more open: "The stuff's all in the
stories; there's no use talking about it."[31]

The response to the "stuff" is what first made Salinger a popular and important writer. From the time
The Catcher in the Rye came out, he was perceived by
his readers—many of whom, we must admit, were
very young—as a writer with a message. The novelist
Joan Didion (*Play It as It Lays*) tells of going to a
party on Bank Street when she first came to New York
in the fall of 1956 and having a Sarah Lawrence girl
declare that Salinger was the only person in the world
capable of understanding her.[32] This level of identification was partly the result of Salinger's strange ability

to make his characters seem so *real* to his audience in
the 1950s. The English critic David Leitch, for example, tells of an American friend calling him in Rome
and telling him that he had met the brother-in-law of
Seymour Glass in a bar and that Leitch should come
down to be introduced. Leitch declined.[33] But the
main reason for the extreme sort of reader identification Salinger elicited is that reading him seemed to
many like a religious experience.

As we look back over Salinger's writing, his concern with religious ecstasy as a means of resolving
personal suffering becomes more and more central.
"The quest upon which his characters are engaged is,
either implicitly or explicitly, a religious one," Kenneth
Hamilton emphasizes in his study of this crucial part
of Salinger's thought. "The situations of stress in which
his young people find themselves drive them always
towards a religious crisis, whether or not this crisis
issues in any type of religious conversion or illumination."[34] His very technique is an indication of the
mystical tendencies that are basic to the eventual
structuring of belief in his fiction. Seldom does anybody do anything directly in a Salinger story. This is a
demonstration of his conviction that reality and truth
must be intuited—they can never be demonstrated.
"The reason for all this play and double-play," Hamilton writes in dealing with Salinger's inscrutability,
"seems to lie in a theory about the communication of
truth taking the following form: that which appears
cannot be that which really is; and therefore only that
which contradicts its surface appearance can open a
way along which the truth may reach us."[35] Salinger
is not a writer who traffics in the obvious.

His religious solutions are not limited to a particular religion; and at times, it is difficult to determine
whether he necessarily has any known religion in
mind. His essential assumption is that religion has to

do with spiritual vision. And while there may be only one religious reality, this reality must be seen, even if only momentarily, through many forms and is not limited to a single faith. In this sense, he is not a Christian writer, even though he has many references to Jesus in his fiction, because historic Christianity attributes spiritual blindness to sin, not just the lack of sensitivity that Salinger repeatedly depicts.

The closest analogue to Salinger's religious thought is, of course, Zen Buddhism, which is essential to an understanding of *Nine Stories* and, apparently, the entire Glass family chronicle. Zen exploits the virtues of nonsense, believing that truth simply cannot be caught by logic. Instead, Zen substitutes "logical nonsense" as a means of penetrating the heart of reality by opening the doors of the senses to that which is beyond sense in search of spiritual joy. Salinger's stories are often thought of as riddles, and this ought to be no surprise since Zen makes use of a peculiar kind of riddle, the *koan*, as a vehicle of its teaching. An example of a *koan* is the question that prefaces *Nine Stories*:

> We know the sound of two hands clapping.
> But what is the sound of one hand clapping?

Contemplation of the riddle is designed to force the mind to the point where reason is unable to divide, separate, and categorize, a point at which enlightenment or *satori* should occur. Salinger's stories should be read with this concept in mind.

But this does not mean that Salinger is advocating that his readers become Buddhists or that he necessarily is one. His many Zen references, as well as his allusions to the *Bhagavad-Gita*, Sri Ramakrishna, Chuang-tzu, *The Way of a Pilgrim*, and the rest are, to a certain extent, as Mizener explains, "only efforts to find alternate ways of expressing what his stories are about."[36] They also serve at least two other purposes. First, Salinger is, at least in part, a satirist, and satire is impossible without a moral basis. And second, while Salinger's choice for his hero is essentially a religious problem, that problem usually boils down to "finding moral integrity, love, and redemption in an immoral world."[37]

Salinger also uses his religious ideas as a means of doing what a good fiction writer must do—disclose character. With Salinger this disclosure is never, finally, one of public character, but is of private character. "The personality is always at grips with a problem which is almost always too strong for it," Donald Barr stresses. "The problem is always love."[38] Salinger's "personalities" all find themselves having to work their way around their own conditional estrangement. Many of them seem literally to think they are in hell, and *The Catcher in the Rye* has as much to do with *The Inferno* as it does with *Huckleberry Finn*. David L. Stevenson states it strongly when he writes, "They are men, women, and adolescents, not trapped by outside fate, but by their own frightened and sometimes tragi-comic awareness of the uncrossable gulf between their need for love and the futility of trying to achieve it on any foreseeable terms."[39] But many of them do achieve it, and this is a wonderful thing in Salinger's stories.

Salinger's role as a religious writer does not mean that he is devoid of what is sometimes called "social statement." In one story, "Blue Melody" (*Cosmopolitan*, September 1948), he deals directly with the problem of race relations by writing about Lida Jones, a black blues singer patterned after Bessie Smith, who dies from appendicitis because the white hospitals to which she is taken will not admit her. And in another story, "A Girl I Knew" (*Good Housekeeping*, February 1948), the narrator returns to Austria after World

War II to learn that the beautiful girl he had loved before the war had been burned up in one of Hitler's incinerators. In most of his stories, at least one social theme seems obvious—he usually presents a conflict between the individual and society with characters trying to move toward a better definition (actually a redefinition in the later dialogues) of the self. But for the most part, French is right in pointing out that Salinger is "concerned with the effects rather than the causes of the human predicament."[40] What he is up to is more of a description of inner life than of social life.

What social commentary there is in Salinger often takes the form of sheer sympathy for the plights of his characters, some of whom in the early stories are downright pathetic. Like so many other American writers, Salinger is full of sentimentality. Growing up at a time when moral attitudes were greatly influenced by the popular song and the lasting effects of the Progressive era, Salinger became much like Dreiser before him and Vonnegut after him, the proponent and perhaps victim of an overwhelming sentimentality, a passion for the wise (and lost) innocence of childhood and the loving security of family life, if not actually for vine-covered cottages. Ihab Hassan has written in his study of the contemporary American novel, *Radical Innocence*, that "if sentimentality means a response more generous than the situation seems objectively to warrant, then Salinger may choose to plead guilty."[41] This is not a defect; it is a valid, even charming, reaction to a world in which sentiment most logically ought to be denied.

In all of this, Salinger takes the reader directly into his confidence. If we read Salinger as a profoundly religious writer whose very sentimentality indirectly leads to social commentary, we soon realize that he has not disappeared at all, even though he has not published anything for a long time. We realize with Paul Levine that, "Without bowing to the popular opiates of sex, violence, and depravity . . . he has quietly managed to present with humor and compassion the most significant and complex moral problems we face today."[42] We realize that he is encouraging us to develop ourselves and to work out our own spiritual emancipation, for it is his idea that we have the power to liberate ourselves from all bondage through enlightenment. We realize that he is less like Fitzgerald, Lardner, or even Rilke, than he is like the philosopher described by Lin Yutang—one "who dreams with one eye open, who views life with love and sweet irony, who mixes his cynicism with a kindly tolerance. . . ."[43] And we finally realize, if we are able to experience his fiction as *satori*, that there is no esoteric doctrine in his teaching, nothing hidden in the closed fist of the teacher.

2

Against Obscenity:
The Catcher in the Rye

The Catcher in the Rye appeared in a sober and realistic time, a period when (by comparison with the 1960s, at any rate) there was a general disenchantment with ideologies, with schemes for the salvation of the world. Salinger's novel, like the decade for which it has become emblematic, begins with the words, "If you really want to hear about it,"[1] words that imply a full, sickening realization that something has happened that perhaps most readers would not want to know about. What we find out about directly in the novel is, of course, what has happened to Salinger's hero-narrator, Holden Caulfield; but we also find out what has happened generally to human ideas on some simple and ultimate questions in the years following World War II. Is it still possible to reconcile self and society? Is it any longer possible to separate the authentic from the phony? What beliefs are essential for survival? What is the role of language in understanding the nature of our reality? Is it possible to create value and endow the universe with meaning? That Salinger deals with these questions in one way or another points to a problem with *The Catcher in the Rye* that has often been ignored or simply not taken seriously—that the climate of ideas surrounding the novel is dense, and that the book is not just the extended and anguished cries of a wise-guy adolescent whose main trouble is that he does not want to grow up.

From the start in *The Catcher in the Rye*, we are struck with the bleakness of Holden Caulfield's life. His existence seems so gratuitous and contingent, so absurd and without apparent meaning that we wonder where Salinger could possibly go with such a story (or why he would want to go any where with it). Holden is so full of despair and loneliness that he is literally nauseated most of the time. He realizes how different he is from other people, yet his own personality barely exists. He is filled with a penetrating nothingness, and for all the advice he gets, no one can tell him what he must do. There is no rational way he can discover a way out of his dilemma, yet he must take action of some sort, and suicide is not it.

In describing Holden's predicament, one cannot avoid using existential platitudes, for Holden is, undoubtedly, in the midst of an existential crisis. Yet for all his despair, Holden is not a character who adequately illustrates the bitter pessimism and seriousness of a character out of the writings of Sartre, nor does he convey the simple message of popular existentialism as suggested by Camus—choose a path, commit yourself, be yourself, realize your own dignity. Salinger conceives of character much the same way Sartre and Camus do, but his use of language, his humor, and his ultimate willingness to look elsewhere for his answers make him a far different writer, even though he begins at the same point: The world with all its obscenities.

The way Holden Caulfield sees the world is stated in the novel's most famous line: "If you had a million years to do it in, you couldn't rub out even half the 'Fuck you' signs in the world" (p. 262). It is ironic that this sentence is the one that is most responsible for the various bannings of the novel in the years following its appearance. The Detroit Police did not understand Salinger's point at all when they pulled the book out of the city's bookstores—that the controversial line, instead of being obscene itself, is directed, as almost all of Salinger's fiction is, *against* obscenity. Holden tries to explain to us not only what is offensive, disgusting, and repulsive to him in human behavior, but also what goes against prevailing notions of modesty and decency. "The things that Holden finds so deeply repulsive are things he calls 'phony,'" writes Dan Wakefield, "and the 'phoniness' in every instance is the absence of love, and, often, the substitution of pretense for love."[2] Holden is a rebel, but he is hardly a rebel without a cause: He begins in a screaming rage against a society of convention, immorality, and the patently false, but he ends by establishing love and acceptance as a saving grace.

When Holden first introduces himself to us, it is difficult to believe that he is going to establish anything. He comes across as the classic screw-up. He has been thrown out of a series of schools, the latest being Pencey Prep in Agerstown, Pennsylvania, and he is undergoing psychiatric treatment in California. A remark by Stradlater, his old roommate at Pencey, seems to pretty well define his character: "You don't do *one damn thing* the way you're supposed to" (p. 53). Holden fails all of his subjects but one (English) his last term at Pencey, he succeeds in alienating himself from the other students, and he even fails as manager of the fencing team (he loses the team equipment on the subway). Yet he is a character type who has his own fascination for the reader. As Arthur Heiserman and James E. Miller, Jr., emphasize, "American literature seems fascinated with the outcast, the person who defies traditions in order to arrive at some pristine knowledge, some personal integrity."[3]

Integrity—or at least frankness—is one of Holden's most engaging qualities as he starts his story with an extended flashback to the day he left Pencey, the kind of school that advertises itself in the back pages of certain magazines with a picture of a guy on a horse jumping over a fence (Holden says that he has never seen a horse anywhere near the place). It is the day of the year's last football game, but Holden goes instead to see "old Spencer," his history teacher, who asked him to stop by before leaving school. Spencer, in a question that echoes throughout the book, asks Holden, "What's the matter with you, boy" (p. 14)? As Spencer tries to lecture him, telling him that he flunked history because he simply did not know anything, Holden's mind wanders to a question of his own, one he returns to time after time in the novel. He wonders what happens to the ducks in the lagoon near Central Park South when winter comes. It is now winter for Holden, and what will happen to him?

Much has been made critically of Holden's obsession with the ducks, and in some ways the symbolism seems too obvious. But the ducks are another one of Salinger's signs, and they suggest a verse from the New Testament: "The foxes have holes and the birds have nests, but the Son of Man has no place to lay his head." Holden, in his perception of the phony, in his outrage against the obscene, and in his own ineptitude is estranged from both his society and nature. He is not, in this respect, a Christ-figure, but he is most certainly a fool for Christ. Once he leaves Pencey, he does not have a place to rest, and his odyssey becomes the story not of a seeker after truth so much as the story of one who seeks relief from his madness through some saving grace, through some healing stroke.

Holden has often been compared to earlier characters in literature. A substantial amount has been written showing his relationship to Huckleberry Finn—a connection that seems obvious enough given the first-person narration, the colloquial language, the emphasis on the problems of adolescence, and the motif of the journey.[4] Holden has also been compared to the hero of Goethe's *The Sorrows of Young Werther*, Byron's Childe Harold in *Childe Harold's Pilgrimage*, and, more significantly, to Fitzgerald's Gatsby in *The Great Gatsby*. The latter point has considerable validity, because both Gatsby and Holden are model characters of innocence and illusion in American literature, and as one critic has stressed, "The central common characteristic of both Gatsby and Holden is the adherence to a powerful, abiding illusion, while around them swirls a corrupt, hostile, essentially phony world."[5] Salinger even goes so far as to have Holden say, "I liked Ring Lardner and *The Great Gatsby* and all. I did, too. I was crazy about *The Great Gatsby*. Old Gatsby. Old sport" (p. 183). Surprising similarities to William Saroyan's *The Human Comedy* (1943) have been noted.[6] In both novels there is an objectionable boy named Ackley, and the name of Saroyan's hero, Homer Macauley, bears some metrical and orthographical similarity to Holden Caulfield. Each of the characters has a sister and two brothers (with one of the brothers either dead or dying), each gets into trouble in a history course, and each has an encounter with a prostitute. But the similarities, as great as they are, end there between Saroyan and Salinger: Holden is a much more memorable character than is Homer Macauley, and *The Catcher in the Rye* is, without argument, a much more important book than is *The Human Comedy*; its story is more subtle, its structure more complex, and its humor more outrageous.

Holden himself suggests another literary comparison that has not been given much emphasis in interpretations of the novel. About half-way through his monologue, Holden says, "If you want to know the truth, the guy I like best in the Bible, next to Jesus, was that lunatic and all, that lived in the tombs and kept cutting himself with stones. I like him ten times as

much as the Disciples, that poor bastard" (p. 130).
Holden *is* the lunatic in the tombs. He lives surrounded by death. One of his obsessions is his younger
brother, Allie, who died from leukemia at the age of
ten. Another one of his obsessions is James Castle, a
boy at one of his former schools, Elkton Hills, who
committed suicide by jumping from a window after
being cruelly harassed by some of the other students.
Holden is also like the lunatic in another way—he
keeps hurting himself as he masochistically puts himself in one situation after another that can only lead to
pain and revulsion. He goes places where he should
not be, he calls up people who do not really want to
see him or even begin to understand him, and he
dwells on thoughts that can only cause him pain. Like
the lunatic, he is possessed by not one demon, but
many (the lunatic's name is "Legion" because of his
multiple possession)—the demon of fate and death,
the demon of emptiness and meaninglessness, the
demon of guilt and condemnation, the demon of
despair, and the demon of jealousy. The casting forth
of these evil spirits is what his story ultimately comes
down to.

The extent of his possession is indicated early in
the book when he learns that his roommate Stradlater's date for the evening is Jane Gallagher, a girl
Holden met the summer before last and with whom he
is vaguely and uncertainly in love. After Stradlater
leaves, Holden sits in his room and begins to think
about what Stradlater might do to Jane. "God, how I
hated him. . . ." Holden later explains. "Most guys at
Pencey just *talked* about having sexual intercourse
with girls all the time—but old Stradlater really did
it. . . . That's the truth" (pp. 55, 63). He is driven by his
jealousy to provoke a fight with Stradlater, who knocks
him down and bloodies his face—the first of several
injuries that Holden manages to inflict on himself in

the course of the novel. But he is unable to stop thinking of Jane and Stradlater, and his own sexual insecurities along with his despair over the obscenity he sees all around him (Stradlater had a way of calmly sweet-talking girls into believing that he actually cared for them) send him off on a self-destructive spiral that, paradoxically, leads to his redemption at the end.

Holden's demonic possession is apparent when he catches the train to New York with the idea of staying in a cheap hotel until the day when his parents expect him home. A lady boards the train at Trenton, notices the Pencey sticker on Holden's luggage, and asks him if he knows her son at the school. Holden automatically adopts another personality. He tells her that his name is Rudolph Schmidt, casually lies to her about how popular and respected her obnoxious son is, and explains his own early departure by saying he is going to have an operation for a brain tumor. He evokes sympathy from her, and she is pleased with what he had said about her son, but it is all deception. In a phony world, phoniness works, but Holden's actions become increasingly those of a madman who seems less and less in control of them.

He goes into a phone booth at Penn Station, but he cannot think of anyone he could reasonably call at that late hour. He gets a cab, mistakenly gives the driver his home address, asks him to turn around, and then asks him if he knows what happened to the ducks in the winter. The driver thinks Holden is nothing more than a wise guy, and drops him off at the Edmont Hotel. Holden checks in, goes up to his room, and finds no comfort in his anonymity and isolation. He looks out his window and watches a transvestite dressing up and parading in front of a mirror in a room on the other side of the hotel. In another window he sees a man and woman squirting water at each other out their mouths. "Sex is something I really don't

understand too hot" (p. 82), he says. He impulsively
decides to call up a woman named Faith Cavendish, a
part-time prostitute, whose number he obtained from
a Princeton student a few months before, and asks her
if she would like to have a drink with him. She offers
to meet him the next day, but he loses his courage and
backs off.

Shaken by his encounters with the inexplicable
and the obscene, he goes down to the bar in the Lav-
ender Room of the hotel and begins to think of his
sister, Phoebe, one of Salinger's infuriatingly precocious children. "You should see her," Holden says.
"You never saw a little kid so pretty and smart in your
whole life" (p. 87). The same age as Allie was when
he died (ten), Phoebe, like him, has had nothing but
A's since she started school. She has learned the dialogue of her favorite movie, *The 39 Steps*, by heart.
And she writes books about a girl detective named
"Hazle" Weatherfield. Phoebe and Allie symbolize
innocence to Holden, but they are more than that. A
major theme in the New Testament is that to enter the
Kingdom of Heaven one must have the purity of heart
that can be achieved only by becoming like little children. Or, as Robert G. Jacobs has stated it, "For Salinger, childhood is the source of the good in human life;
it is in that state that human beings are genuine and
open in their love for one another. It is when people
become conscious in their relationships to one another,
become adults, that they become 'phony' and logical
and come to love the reasons for love more than the
loved person."[7]

That Holden himself sees childhood as the source
of good in human life is indicated in the title of the
novel. At one point in his wanderings through New
York, he sees a father, a mother, and their six-year-old
son who had all apparently just come out of church.
The parents are talking to one another, paying no at-

tention to the child who is walking in the street, next to the curb, with traffic zooming by dangerously close. Disturbed and fascinated by the scene, Holden gets close enough to hear the boy singing a song, "If a body catch a body coming through the rye." Late that night he sneaks into his parents' apartment to see Phoebe and tries to explain to her why he has left school by saying that he did not like anything that was happening at Pencey. She replies by suggesting that perhaps his problem is just that—that he does not like *anything*, that he does not want to become *anything* (a lawyer, for instance, like his father), and that he does not want to do *anything*. Holden pauses, and then he tells her what he would like to be. He asks her if she knows the song the boy in the street was singing. Wise child that she is, she of course knows that it is a poem by Robert Burns and, furthermore, that Holden has the words wrong. It actually goes, "If a body meet a body coming through the rye"—a significant difference, because it indicates Holden's subconscious desire to "rewrite," to change an order of things that he finds unacceptable. His reply to Phoebe is one of the most famous passages in the novel:

"I thought it was 'If a body catch a body,'" I said. "Anyway, I keep picturing all these little kids playing some game in this big field of rye and all. Thousands of little kids, and nobody's around—nobody big, I mean—except me. And I'm standing on the edge of some crazy cliff. What I have to do, I have to catch everybody if they start to go over the cliff—I mean if they're running and they don't look where they're going I have to come out from somewhere and *catch* them. That's all I'd do all day. I'd just be the catcher in the rye and all. I know it's crazy, but that's the only thing I'd really like to be. I know it's crazy." (p. 225)

The "fall" he is talking about is the fall from the innocence of childhood into the obscenity of adulthood.

Holden, in his anger at the phoniness of Pencey Prep
and other institutions imposed upon the young by the
old, wants a world populated by sweet children whose
skates need lacing and by nuns who can teach English
literature and be untouched by the sexual overtones in
it.

The problem with all of this for Holden is that he
is sixteen; he cannot remain a child—he cannot stand
at the edge of the cliff and be the catcher; he must fall
off into adulthood. But there are ways to fall and ways
not to fall, a lesson that is pointed out to Holden after
he sneaks back out of the apartment and goes to visit
Mr. Antolini, his old English teacher at Elkton Hills
and now an instructor at N. Y. U. Mr. Antolini cannot
approve of Holden's behavior, and tells him, in a
thematic echo of the wish to be the catcher in the rye
that Holden expresses to Phoebe, that Holden is riding
for a fall. "This fall I think you're riding for—it's a
special kind of fall, a horrible kind," Mr. Antolini explains. "The man falling isn't permitted to feel or hear
himself hit bottom. He just keeps falling and falling.
The whole arrangement's designed for men who, at
some time or other in their lives, were looking for
something their own environment couldn't supply
them with. So they gave up looking. They gave it up
before they ever really even got started" (p. 244). In
other words, one may fall into disillusionment, giving
up on the possibilities in life as the innocent dreams of
childhood are by necessity abandoned. Or one may
break the fall, may even land, by realizing that indeed
there are things one's environment simply cannot supply, such as innocence, selfless love, freedom from
obscenity.

Mr. Antolini expands his lecture to Holden by
reading him a quotation from Wilhelm Stekhel, a
psychoanalyst who was the colleague of Freud and
Jung and the author of numerous works expressing

his theories on the relationship between infantilism and maturity.[8] " 'The mark of the immature man is that he wants to die nobly for a cause,' " Mr. Antolini cites, " 'while the mark of the mature man is that he wants to live humbly for one' " (p. 244). Holden's immaturity on this point is apparent: As the catcher in the rye, he sees himself risking his own life (in fact denying it through his refusal to grow up and through his wish to keep other children from doing so) on the edge of the "crazy cliff." His conception is an over-dramatized vision of himself as a "savior," nobly sacrificing himself for the sake of preserving what he takes to be the innocent and the good. What he needs is to find something he can *live* for, instead of something he wants to die for.

At the center of Holden's difficulties is the dangerous symbolism of childhood and its innocence. His disgust with the adult world is so great that he is blinded to the realities of childhood. Infantile sexuality was once considered one of the most shocking aspects of Freudian thought. And one does not have to be a social worker to know that children often delight in writing the words on walls that Holden finds so offensive. Even Phoebe is depicted as being much more worldly than Holden perceives her as being. For example, she indicates that she knows quite clearly what is going on when a boy in her class, Curtis Weintraub, persists in following her around. What Holden must come to understand is that the scriptures do not say that one can become a child again—or even that it is ever possible, even when a child, to be what the word implies. Sin and corruption are too much with us from the day we are born. But we can become *like* a child in believing in the *possibility* of goodness despite the obscenity that surrounds us.

Coming to such a realization is by no means easy, for even in the midst of truth one must deal with

corruption. Holden's experience with Mr. Antolini is
a case in point. Mr. Antolini illuminates Holden's life,
but Mr. Antolini's own life is representative of the kind
of "maturity" that is shallow and phony in itself. He
has married an older woman for her money, and it is
apparent that he does not love her. He is an alcoholic,
and he is drunk when he is talking to Holden. His
practical suggestion concerning Holden's future is a
lame and unthinking defense of "applying" oneself in
school and pursuing a conventional academic career.
And in the middle of the night, as Holden is asleep on
the couch, Mr. Antolini makes a homosexual advance
toward him. All of this provides Holden with an em-
blem of what the adult world he has fallen into is
like—the true and the obscene all mixed together.
"The more I thought about it, though, the more de-
pressed and screwed up about it I got" (p. 253), he
concludes when he wakes up the next morning in the
waiting room of Grand Central Station.

Thought is not going to be any help to him. When
he first starts talking to Mr. Antolini, he indicates that,
subconsciously at least, he senses this. He is trying to
explain to Mr. Antolini why he flunked his class in oral
expression at Pencey. The teacher, Mr. Vinson, spent
most of his time arguing the importance of sticking to
the point and avoiding digression. The trouble with
this idea, Holden maintains, is that he likes listening to
a speech better when someone digresses. He says this
of Mr. Vinson: "He could drive you crazy sometimes,
him and the goddam class. I mean he'd keep telling
you to *uni*fy and *simp*lify all the time. Some things you
just can't *do* that to" (p. 240). The same thing is true
of Holden's own story—it is not unified and simplified;
it is in itself an extended digression leading in fits and
starts toward a moment of illumination that is not the
result of logical, ordered thought.

This has made for problems in reading *The*

Catcher in the Rye, because the logic of the conclusion is present only metaphorically. Like the lunatic in the tombs, Holden goes through an exorcism that works, but he is not quite certain how it has worked. He leaves the waiting room and is suddenly surrounded by the trappings of Christmas—Santa Clauses on every streetcorner and displays in the stores. As he walks, he sees some workmen unloading a Christmas tree off a truck, one of them saying to the other, "Hold the sonuvabitch *up!* Hold it *up,* for Chrissake!" (p. 255). Holden starts to laugh and then he is overcome by nausea—his dual reaction to the duality of the world. As the humor in his monologue shows, Holden perceives the comic nature of human life, yet this comedy is often the result of a depressing juxtaposition of the sacred and the profane, a juxtaposition that is central to Salinger's art. As Ihab Hassan has stressed, "Revulsion and holiness make up the rack on which Salinger's art still twitches."[9] How to maintain a sense of the holy in the midst of obscenity is what Holden's character development is all about.

As he walks up Fifth Avenue, he experiences an hallucination that brings together all of his anxieties at once. Every time he comes to the end of a block and steps off the curb, he has the feeling that he will never get to the other side of the street; he will fall off the curb and disappear. He begins to pray to his brother, Allie, not to let him disappear. In the midst of his anxieties over fate and death, emptiness and meaninglessness, guilt and condemnation, and despair, he appeals to Allie to save him, yet the memories of Allie and the seeming sacrilege of his death embody all of those anxieties in themselves. What he is actually praying for is a means of saving himself from himself through himself.

He rests for a time sweating on a park bench and thinks about escaping by hitchhiking out west and get-

ting a job working at a filling station. He would pre-
tend to be a deaf-mute so he would not have to talk to
anyone, and he would live by himself out in the woods
in a log cabin. This is both a theme and a means of
escape that runs through American literature—and
through the adolescent mind. Holden, in what turns
out to be the last gasp of his rebellion, buys the idea.
He decides that he will go away, that he would never
go home again, and that he would never go to another
school. But first he must say good-by to Phoebe. He
goes to her school and leaves a note telling her that he
is leaving town and that she should meet him at the
Museum of Natural History at quarter past twelve if
she can.

While he is waiting for her, he goes into his favorite room in the Museum—the mummies' tomb. He
likes the room because it is always the same, just as he
would like his world to be (it is significant that the
only thing that interested him in his history course at
Pencey is the ancient Egyptians' secret of preserva-
tion). But then, in what leads to a moment of revelation, he notices an obscenity written with a child's red
crayon on the wall. "That's the whole trouble," he finally realizes. "You can't ever find a place that's nice
and peaceful, because there isn't any. You may *think*
there is, but once you get there, when you're not looking, somebody'll sneak up and write 'Fuck you' right
under your nose" (p. 264). He even concludes that
when he dies, someone will write "Fuck you" on his
tombstone. Right away he is sickened and goes to the
toilet, where he passes out and falls to the floor. This
fall, which results from his realization of the essential
obscenity of life itself, is the one he has been dread-
ing, the fall from adolescence into adulthood. But he
survives, although he is not sure why. "I was lucky,
though," he says. "I mean I could've killed myself when
I hit the floor, but all I did was sort of land on my

side. It was a funny thing, though. I felt better after I passed out. I really did" (p. 265).

This is a lucky fall, a "fortunate" fall. Only through coming to terms with the fallen nature of the world through his own fall can Holden achieve release. And in the next scene, when he goes to the zoo with Phoebe and sits on a bench in the park watching her ride the carousel, we see that he has left his idea of being the catcher in the rye behind. "All the kids kept trying to grab for the gold ring, and so was old Phoebe," he says quietly, "and I was sort of afraid she'd fall off the goddam horse, but I didn't say anything or do anything. The thing with kids is, if they want to grab for the gold ring, you have to let them do it, and not say anything. If they fall off, they fall off, but it's bad if you say anything to them" (p. 274). And suddenly Holden is surrounded by symbols that suggest rebirth, blessing, and hopefulness. It is raining, it is Christmas, and in the carousel's circular movement he obtains a true and vital vision of eternity to replace his old lunatic's love for the mummies' tomb.

In the epilogue, we learn that Holden did finally go home, that he got sick, and that he wound up out in California in the psychiatric ward—an ending that at first seems to be another digression or, much worse, that contradicts the joyous scene at the zoo with Phoebe and the carousel. But the final chapter works to show the progress Holden has made in moving toward authenticity and understanding the essential question that is behind every good novel: What is the nature of reality? The answer resides in the dynamic relationship between childhood and maturity, between the static and the changeable, between thought and action, and between the outer and inner worlds—a reality that is "an existentialist datum of physical and emotional experience."[10] This datum, which has its immediate basis in Christian thought, finds its ultimate rationale in Buddhism—a crucial point in understanding the end of the novel, an ending that points directly to *Nine Stories*.

One of the mistakes in reading *The Catcher in the Rye* is to assume, since Holden is under the treatment of a psychoanalyst, that the novel closes with some unsettled psychoanalytical questions concerning Holden's experiences and his future. This is not the case at all. Holden has been sick, but he has already been cured, and the resources of his personality are strong at the end, so strong that it is he, not the psychoanalyst, who possesses the insights. This can be seen in the three seemingly puzzling statements he makes in the final chapter. The first is when he responds to the doctor's question of whether or not he is going to apply himself when he goes back to school, by saying, "I mean how do you know what you're going to do till you *do* it?" (p. 276). The second is when his brother, D. B., asks him what he thinks about the story he has just finished telling, and Holden replies, "If you want to know the truth, I don't *know* what I think about it" (pp. 276–277). And the third is when he ends by saying that he misses everybody he told about, even the pimp who beat him up after a pathetic encounter with a prostitute at the Edmont Hotel, and adds, "Don't ever tell anybody anything. If you do, you start missing everybody" (p. 277). The meaning of these statements may be puzzling, but their purpose is not: They are intended as Zen riddles or *koan*, designed to present intellectual impasses that serve to indicate, sharpen, and define the elusiveness and indefinability of life. As Alan W. Watts explains it in *The Way of Zen*, "when the disciple comes to the final point where the *koan* absolutely refuses to be grasped, he comes also to the realization that life can never be grasped, never possessed or made to stay still. Whereupon he 'lets go,' and this letting go is the acceptance of life *as* life. . . ."[11] This is the insight, the illumination Holden has reached by the time his story is over and he has left his precept-laden anxieties behind.

Holden is thus not, as many of Salinger's critics have maintained, a tragic figure, a victim of modern society. He is not mentally defeated at the end, and he has surprisingly come to terms with the world in which he must live. Salinger's gospel is a positive one, showing "how exposure of the sensitive soul to the darkness of this present age can lead not only to sickness but also to healing."[12]

What actually happens to Holden Caulfield as he moves from sickness to health in *The Catcher in the Rye* was not understood by most reviewers when the novel came out. Given the reputation and huge sales the book eventually achieved, it is surprising to look at the early reviews and discover that so many of them were negative, and quite a few even hostile. Jocelyn Brooke, writing in *The New Statesman and Nation*, was something of an exception, coming close to describing the novel as it is: "This is an odd, tragic, and at times an appallingly funny book, with a taste of its own."[13] The opinion of R. D. Charques in *The Spectator* is more typical: "Intelligent, humorous, acute and sympathetic in observation, the tale is rather too formless to do quite the sort of thing it was evidently intended to do."[14] And in a direct attack on the book, Anne L. Goodman expresses an opinion she shared with a number of other critics in 1951: "the book as a whole is disappointing, and not merely because it is a reworking of a theme that one begins to suspect must obsess the author."[15]

Salinger's obsession with adolescent angst did

cause considerable comment, and he did have his
defenders. The poet Paul Engle, for example, saw the
story as "an engaging and believable one for the most
part, full of right observations and sharp insight, and a
wonderful sort of grasp of how a boy can create his
own world of fantasy and live form."[16] Harrison
Smith, commenting in *The Saturday Review of Literature*, described the novel as a "profoundly moving and
. . . disturbing book."[17] And Clifton Fadiman, in a
report that appeared in the *Book of the Month Club
News*, stated that "The pleasantest task your Editorial
Board can undertake is the sponsoring of a brilliant,
new, young American novelist such as Mr. Salinger.
Perhaps, come to think of it, 'brilliant' is an unsatisfactory adjective, for one may be brilliant and have little
to say. Brilliance is born merely of a smooth reflecting
surface. Mr. Salinger, however, reflects in both senses:
he has polish *and* depth. His book arouses our imagination—but more to the point, it starts flowing in us
the clear springs of pity, understanding, and affec-
tionate laughter."[18]

But despite the praise the novel did receive and
despite its success as a Book of the Month Club selection, it was looked upon by many readers as a potentially dangerous, even seditious, book. The character
of Holden Caulfield was hardly the kind of model parents wanted for their children. "Fortunately, there
cannot be many of him yet," T. Morris Longstreth
wrote with apprehension in *The Christian Science
Monitor*, "But one fears that a book like this given
wide circulation may multiply his kind—as too easily
happens when immorality and perversion are re-
counted by writers of talent whose work is coun-
tenanced in the name of art or good intention."[19] This
reaction, based on a misreading of the novel that is
now difficult to understand (Salinger is making a

strong statement *against* immorality and perversion), was hardly confined to the pages of the *Monitor*.

A review in *Catholic World* centers on an objection that soon became the pivotal point in the controversy over *The Catcher in the Rye* and its being banned in bookshops, libraries, and schools across the United States: "Not only do some of the events stretch probability, but Holden's character as iconoclast, a kind of latter-day Tom Sawyer or Huck Finn, is made monotonous and phony by the formidably excessive use of amateur swearing and coarse language."[20] Again and again, reviewers, critics, and general readers passed over the essentially moral and religious themes of the book to profess shock at the language. For some, of course, it was not the language itself that was so disturbing, it was that Salinger puts the words in the mouth of a sixteen-year-old boy. As Virgilia Peterson explained, in making just such a comment about the book in the *New York Herald Tribune Book Review*, "Recent war novels have accustomed us all to ugly words and images, but from the mouths of the very young and protected they sound peculiarly offensive. There is probably not one phrase in the whole book that Holden Caulfield would not have used upon occasion, but when they are piled upon each other in cumulative monotony, the ear refuses to believe."[21]

It is Salinger's use of language that is one of the most distinctive qualities of *The Catcher in the Rye*, and an analysis of that language is essential to an appreciation of just what Salinger accomplishes artistically in the novel. If we look at the language in isolation, it is crude, profane, and obscene—by the standards of most people even in 1979 as well as in 1951. But if we look at the language and its relationship to the overall effect of the novel, another conclusion emerges. "Given the point of view from which the novel is told," Edward P. J. Corbett argues in a sensible article on the whole matter of *The Catcher in the Rye* and censorship, "and given the kind of character that figures as the hero, no other language was possible. The integrity of the novel demanded such language."[22] It is not simply a matter of realizing that Holden's language would not seem at all unusual or shocking to a real-life prep-school boy. His swearing is habitual and so unconsciously ritualistic that it contributes to, rather than diminishes, the theme of innocence that runs through the novel. In addition, Holden is characterized by a "desperate bravado"[23]—he wants to appear older than he is, and his rough language fits in with his concept of the corrupt adult world.

Holden's way of talking is, it must be realized, a device. Salinger is not directly interested in merely depicting the way a boy like Holden would actually speak—no more than Mark Twain was attempting to be "realistic" in the literal sense when he invented an idiom for Huckleberry Finn (an important thing to remember here is that Twain's novel, like Salinger's, was widely castigated for its language and even banned because of it). "Neither J. D. Salinger nor Mark Twain really 'copied' anything," Heiserman and Miller remind us. "Their books would be unreadable had they merely recorded intact the language of a real-life Huck and a real-life Holden. Their genius lies in their mastery of the technique of first-person narration which, through meticulous selection, creates vividly the illusion of life: gradually and subtly their narrators emerge and stand revealed, stripped to their innermost beings."[24] Or, as Mary McCarthy has observed, "The artless dialect is an artful ventriloquial trick of Salinger's, like the deliberate halting English of Hemingway's waiters, fishermen, and peasants—anyone who speaks it is a good guy, a friend of the author's, to be trusted."[25]

Salinger's genius does derive in large part from his ability as a literary ventriloquist. He is a writer concerned with messages, with stressing moral points and suggesting ways to move from despair to illumination. Holden Caulfield thus comes to embody Salinger's thought, but the language Salinger chooses to give him is so artfully controlled that the voice seems to come from some other source than the author. The problem a ventriloquist must always get around is to make his audience forget that the figure on his knee is just a wooden dummy, not "real," and this is what Salinger succeeds in doing in *The Catcher in the Rye*—something that does not always happen in his later work, where it is often all too apparent that he is carrying on a pretended conversation with characters who are only lovable puppets.

But even though Holden's language is artful pretense, it never seems pretended. Donald P. Costello in his thorough and insightful study of Salinger's use of language in the novel has uncovered some of the reasons why this is so.[26] First of all, Salinger does know enough about authentic teenage speech to establish a basic level of believability that he never departs from in the novel. Holden never says anything that he conceivably could not have said. Salinger manages, however, to individualize Holden through having him make use of certain repetitions in an unusually significant way. Like other teenagers of his time and place, Holden repeats *and all* and *I really did*, as well as the famous, *if you want to know the truth*. But these repetitions have a purpose beyond simple realism. Holden repeats *I really did* to establish that he is not a phony. He repeats *and all* because of his eventual mystic ability to find the all in the one as he moves toward his final vision. And he repeats *if you want to know the truth* because that is what the book at last is about.

A second point about Salinger's language is that

Holden's speech at first seems to be typical schoolboy
vulgarity. But a closer look reveals that it is actually
restrained to indicate Holden's sensitivity. After all,
Holden is offended by certain uses of coarse language.
The word *fuck* appears four times, but it is never a
part of Holden's speech. Holden uses *goddam* often,
but never the more offensive *Jesus Christ* or even *for
Chrissake* except in repeating the speech of others.
One soon notices that the crudity of language in-
creases when Holden is reporting what others say and
decreases significantly when he directly addresses the
reader.

A third point concerns something Salinger has in
common with Sinclair Lewis—his love for slang words
and expressions. But unlike Lewis's work, Salinger's
does not seem strikingly dated in its reliance on jar-
gon, because the slang words Salinger selects are nar-
row in choice and carefully repeated—words like
lousy, pretty, crumby, terrific, quite, old, and *stupid.*
The repetition of identical words and expressions in
different situations is, however, humorous and also
shows the American characteristic of adapting nouns
into adjectives and nouns into adverbs. He turns nouns
into adverbs simply by adding a *y,* and we have
vomity-looking, show-offy, pimpy, and *perverty.* Perhaps more distinctive is his ability to use nouns as
adverbs: "She sings it very Dixieland and whorehouse,
and it doesn't sound at all mushy" (p. 149).

But Holden is no mere illiterate adolescent. He
reveals his education in the way he discourses on two
levels at once. He uses, for example, the colloquial
take a leak at one time and then the more genteel
relieve himself at another—a shift in word-choice that
contributes to the humor in the novel. Like a typical
kid his age might do, Holden does violate some rules
of grammar. He consistently misuses *lie* and *lay,* is
uncertain about relative pronouns, and is a devotee of

the double negative. But he is extremely conscious of his own speech and is especially critical of the language of others. His character builds through this consciousness, and his eventual self-awareness is made more acceptable through his ability to recognize the phony, the untrue, in his objections to the overuse of such words as *grand, prince, traveling incognito,* and *little girls' room.* And it is often forgotten that Holden, in revealing his character, is *speaking,* not writing. If he were writing, his grammatical mistakes would be fewer and he would never write so many fragments.

A close look at the language in *The Catcher in the Rye* leads to a conclusion stated memorably by Costello: "The language of *The Catcher in the Rye* is an authentic rendering of a type of informal, colloquial, teenage American spoken speech. It is strongly typical and trite, yet often somewhat individual; it is crude and slangy and imprecise, imitative yet occasionally imaginative, and affected toward standardization by the strong efforts of schools. But authentic and interesting as this language may be, it must be remembered that it exists . . . as only one part of an artistic achievement."[27] But it is certainly a powerful part of Salinger's artistry and is a reminder of how careful a writer he is. His relatively small output is not due to a limited imagination; it is more likely due to his extreme care in choosing the words he is going to use.

Salinger's attitudes toward language further suggest a conceptual relationship between him and the philosopher of what was called the school of Linguistic Analysis, Ludwig Wittgenstein (1889–1951), an Austrian who did much of his work at Oxford University. Wittgenstein concluded that there is no discoverable reality outside of language, that we live in a world of words that is much more important to us than the illusory world of facts we think we live in. He reached the point where he even argued that the human desire to understand the world is an outdated folly because there is an impenetrable veil between the world of words and the world of fact. Wittgenstein's ideas are hardly easy and they cannot be easily applied to Salinger, but Holden Caulfield does live in a world of words, and the memory one has of *The Catcher in the Rye* is less of what Holden describes about the world of facts than of how his description is in itself a world of words.

An interesting sidenote about Wittgenstein is that his development and personality bear some resemblance to Salinger's. Wittgenstein was austere and ascetic, known for his integrity and, after he gave up professing at Oxford, achieved a reputation as something of an intellectual saint. He began as an engineering student, but he moved from science to philosophy through the study of religion. In the years after World War I, Wittgenstein was greatly influenced by Tolstoy's religious writings and became a simple village schoolmaster, even thinking about becoming a monk (one thinks of Holden's question to Ackley about what it takes to join a monastery).

But whatever the relationship between the two, both Salinger and Wittgenstein, in line with contemporary "structuralist" linguistics, stress the importance of language dimensions in understanding the nature of reality. We are, they both seem to agree, the prisoners of our language, an irrational structure from which we cannot escape. We think largely as language directs us to think, a process we can observe clearly as we read *The Catcher in the Rye*. Holden is so dominated by his language that he *is*, indeed, his language. He is deposited in a strange world of which he can make no sense and from which he seems cut off. But through his scrutiny of language, through his scrutiny of the structure that *thinks him*, he plays a series of word games that endow his condition with meaning. This is what the *koans* at the end of the book come down to. And a good part of Salinger's achievement in the novel is the way the book works to elucidate the language of everyday life.

The climate of ideas surrounding *The Catcher in the Rye* is, as even a brief consideration of the theories of language in the novel suggests, more dense, more diverse, than was realized when the book was published. While it is dangerous to argue that *The Catcher in the Rye* derives from any particular earlier work or school of thought, it does, in many ways, embody the general intellectual interests of the 1950s. There was, for instance, considerable interest in anthropology and psychology in the decade. Margaret Mead's *Coming of Age in Samoa* (1928) and Ruth Benedict's *Patterns of Culture* (1934) became popular and influential when they appeared as paperbacks after World War II. Depth psychology, with its emphasis on the unconscious and the impact of myth, ritual, and archetype on the theory of instincts and man's primordial nature, shows up in Joseph Campbell's *The Hero with a Thousand Faces* (1949), C. G. Jung's *Psychology and Alchemy* (1953), Lionel Trilling's *Freud and the Crisis of Our Culture* (1955), and Otto Rank's *The Myth and Birth of the Hero* (1959). Holden Caulfield's story is not only told against a background of myth and archetype (like Ulysses, he is on a quest, and at the end of the novel we see him going through a symbolic death and resurrection), it is also an anthropological study of the rites of passage from adolescence into adulthood for an American youth of Holden's type.

It has often been assumed that, because of the internalization of plot in *The Catcher in the Rye*, the novel is not much of a reflection of its times nor much of a commentary on the society from which it emerges. Maxwell Geismar makes such an objection when he writes, "Just as the hero's interest in the ancient Egyptians extends only to the fact that they created mummies, so Salinger's own view of his hero's environment omits any reference to its real nature and dynamics."[28] This is hardly the case. *The Catcher in the Rye* should be seen as one of many books published in the postwar era that serve as significant cultural criticism of conformity in a mass society. Alfred Kinsey in his two works, works that were even more controversial than *The Catcher in the Rye*, *Sexual Behavior of the American Male* (1948) and *Sexual Behavior of the American Female* (1953), raises, through statistical study, the whole question of sexual normality. Holden's concern over still being a virgin at age sixteen and his admission that his sexual experience has been retarded would have been seen against the background of the Kinsey report by Salinger's readers in the 1950s. The same thing is true of Salinger's indirect but nonetheless constant commentary on how money is made and how success is achieved in America. Holden's attitude toward D. B.'s sell-out to Hollywood, his reluctance to even consider becoming a lawyer like his father, and the ridicule he directs at the distinguished Pencey alumnus who made a fortune through establishing a chain of cut-rate funeral parlors, all point toward similar criticisms of American democracy in C. Wright Mill's *White Collar* (1951) and *The Power Elite* (1956), William H. Whyte's *The Organization Man* (1956), Vance Packard's *The Hidden Persuaders* (1957), and John Kenneth Galbraith's *The Affluent Society* (1958).

But of all the books of this sort, the one that is most closely tied to *The Catcher in the Rye* is David Riesman's *The Lonely Crowd* (1950). Like Salinger, Riesman deals with the peculiar and often contradictory pressures to conform exerted upon the individual by a mass society. Riesman invented two terms that were very much discussed during the 1950s—"inner direction" and "outer direction." The first term indicates the character taught to children in the nineteenth century when the most important social aim was production. At a time when most goods were produced by individuals or small manufacturers, self-reliance, self assurance, and an inflexible set of principles were the necessary virtues for success. The puritan ethic is an example. As Riesman writes, "the source of direction for the individual is 'inner' in the sense that it is implanted early in life by the elders and directed toward generalized but nonetheless inescapably destined goals."[29] But since about 1920, the productive process has been taken over by machines owned by giant corporations. Success suddenly demanded a more flexible and compromising personality. The nineteenth-century man who took pride in being able "to go it on his own" and "to be as honest as the day is long" had little place in the executive structure of a manufacturing conglomerate. What was needed was someone who could "play the game," who could "get along with others," who could "fit in." This person was "other-directed" in that others, his contemporaries, his friends, neighbors, and business associates are his source of direction, and his goals shift as the signals he picks up from others shift. The social pressures that serve to create an "other-directed" personality are reinforced by economic pressures to be a good consumer of what the machines have produced. Being a good consumer means being sensitive to one's neighbors; keeping up with the Joneses means becoming aware of whatever new consumer product is going to bring status. And this, of course, makes the "other-directed" person especially vulnerable to the mass media, which is constantly redefining which product, which style, which look, and even which ideas are the most prestigious.

While Riesman does not argue that the "other-directed" personality is necessarily bad for the future of civilization and that a return to the rigidity of nineteenth-century values is desirable, he does develop a conception of modern corporate society into which the dilemma of Holden Caulfield fits. One of Riesman's main concerns in *The Lonely Crowd* is with the difficulties "other direction" brought on in child raising. "Inner direction" implied certainties in the spheres of work and social relations that made bringing up children easier. Children were once raised to move easily and without trauma from childhood into adulthood, from the world of play into the world of work, because their play was directed toward production, and where it stopped being play and suddenly became work was undefinable. The blacksmith's son begins, for example, by playing in the shop, and soon he is helping. An important point to consider here is that in the nineteenth century, the ideas of "teenager" and "adolescent" were not at all current. But in an "other-directed" society, the movement from childhood to adulthood is seldom a smooth one because there is a built-in dissonance.

Without an "inner direction" to implant in their children, parents are forced to encourage them to develop "outer direction" through extensive and "permissive" contact with other children from nursery school and even earlier. Just how early was emphasized in Dr. Benjamin Spock's best-selling *Baby and Child Care* (1946). Spock taught that there are no problem children, only problem parents, and he repudiated the rigid schedules that almost all previous child-care books had endorsed. Instead, he claimed that children should be fed according to their own rhythms. They should not be taught certain skills, such as reading and writing, until they are ready. And it is important that they be given the opportunity to learn from each other, not only from authority figures. The result was the "open" classroom where children supposedly developed their personalities in a relaxed and friendly atmosphere with the teachers serving as opinion leaders.

One difficulty eventually comes up, however. The new approach to child-raising and education tried, as much as possible, to keep children free from rigid timetables. But the corporation cannot allow people to remain children for long; it can permit permissiveness only up to a point. Eventually it is no longer socially functional to encourage independence. Sooner or later, the child will be asked to join an economic system that is rigidly defined, that is run according to timeclocks, working days, and production quotas. But what if the children do not want to? What if they rebel? What if they refuse to become organization men? When that happens, a character like Holden Caulfield emerges.

Holden refuses to relate to others the way his society with its idea of "other direction" would have him do. He refuses to go to the football game and cheer his heart out for old Pencey the way most of his fellow students do. He refuses to participate in his classes the way he is expected to. He rejects the attitudes toward sex that he is supposed to learn from the more experienced Stradlater. And he buys and wears a red deer-hunting cap not because it is the fashion or because he has been encouraged by advertising to buy it; he wears it simply because *he* thinks he looks good in it. He is uncomfortable in his twentieth-century social setting and the demands it places on him, and it is his desire to return to the older, "inner-directed" world (his dream is to go out west and live in a log cabin the way people used to do in the nineteenth century). He cannot actually do this, but his enlightenment and apparent peace at the end is the result of an "inner" process that leads to a way of resisting the conformity that his parents, his schools, and his doctors have been trying to encourage him to accept.

Holden's suspicion of and final rejection of "other-directed" society can be seen no better than in his sarcasm concerning movies in the novel. Holden indicates that he likes to read, and lists a fairly impressive selection of favorite books ranging from Thomas Hardy's *The Return of the Native* to Isak Dinesen's *Out of Africa*. Reading is associated with the era of inner-direction; it is something Holden does all by himself. Movie-going is another matter. Even if one attends alone, the viewing is a communal matter. The experience itself depends on the reactions of other people in the audience; it is a matter of "other direction." Holden's dislike of the movies is not so much of the films themselves as it is of the way he sees other people reacting to them. He is relieved when he does not have to go to the movie with Brossard and Ackley the night he leaves Pencey. "I didn't care about not seeing the movie, anyway," he explains. "It was supposed to be a comedy with Cary Grant in it, and all that crap. Besides, I'd been to the movies with Brossard and Ackley before. They both laughed like hyenas at stuff that wasn't even funny. I didn't even enjoy sitting next to them in the movies" (p. 48). His reaction is much the same when, to kill some time the next day in New York, he goes to the movies at Radio City. The movie, he says, is "putrid" but what really bothers him is that the woman sitting next to him cries all the way through it. "The phonier it got, the more she cried," he complains. "You'd have thought she did it because she was kindhearted as hell, but I was sitting right next to her, and she wasn't. She had this little kid with her that was bored as hell and had to go to the bathroom, but she wouldn't take him. She kept telling him to sit still and behave himself. She was about as kindhearted as a goddam wolf. You take somebody that cries their goddam eyes out over phony stuff in the movies, and nine times out of ten they're mean bastards at heart. I'm not kidding" (p. 181).

In his suspicions of the movies and other forms of other-directed mass media, Holden is a rebel against what he takes to be a life-threatening phoniness in his society. His suspicion can be seen as part of the generalized paranoia that accompanied the McCarthy era, the Korean War, and the fear of atomic attack that produced the so-called "silent generation" of gray-flannel conformists. But Holden is not silent. His monologue is a noisy one that proclaims an alternative, a way of defying and even escaping from other-directed mass society by learning to perceive reality from the inside, by learning how to find meaning from within.

The influence of Holden's example on an entire generation of readers is impossible to measure, but it is difficult to ignore in considering the development of the "counterculture" of white American youth in the 1960s. The conventional virtues they rejected—competitive masculinity, military supremacy, and the emphasis on self discipline in order to channel energy into economic achievement—are all virtues rejected by Holden. And the belief that non-Western thought could provide humanizing answers that centuries of Christianity and European philosophy had not is as much a part of Salinger and *The Catcher in the Rye* as it is of the Beat movement. Like Gary Snyder, Salinger suggests the use of Zen Buddhism as a means of discipline necessary to cleanse the mind of certain untruths promoted by mass culture in America. Holden Caulfield's long digression is a pilgrimage to find meaning, one he has doubtless encouraged others to follow on the path back to a revitalized sense of inner direction.

But however extensive the influence of Salinger's most notorious character, he is a major reason for Salinger's fame and popularity. In the real and relevant idiom of Holden, Salinger caught and dissected modern society through a symbolic structure of language, motif, and episode that is as masterful as anything in contemporary literature. *The Catcher in the Rye* is a novel that fights obscenity with an amazing and divine mixture of vulgarity and existential anguish, and it does this through a style that moves the narrative effortlessly along on a colloquial surface that suddenly parts to reveal the terror and beauty of the spiritual drama that Holden enacts. It may be Salinger's only novel, but it is still one of the best we have.

3

Zen Art and
Nine Stories

The secret of balancing form with emptiness and in knowing when one has said enough is behind the art of the modern short story. This secret is also behind the art forms of Zen Buddhism with its emphasis on an idea that must be at the center of every good short story: One showing is worth a hundred sayings. The short-story writer and the Zen artist must work to convey the impression of unhesitating spontaneity, realizing that a single stroke is enough to give away character, and avoiding filling in the essential empty spaces with explanation, second thoughts, and intellectual commentary. These principles are brought together in Salinger's *Nine Stories*, a collection of his finest work and a startling blend of West and East in its aesthetic assumptions.

Salinger is undoubtedly a better short-story writer than he is a novelist. His development as a writer can be traced back to Whit Burnett's course in the techniques of the short story at Columbia University in 1939, and Salinger has hinted that he has learned from the examples of Ring Lardner, F. Scott Fitzgerald, and even Hemingway. In language and tone, most of his early stories clearly, sometimes embarrassingly, show such influences. But the pieces he collected for *Nine Stories* reveal an artistic purpose (one could even say a philosophy of composition) that certainly sets Salinger apart from his older models. It is not that his stories depart so much in structure from those of other writers. What happens in the short stories of Chekhov or Joyce also happens in the short stories of Salinger—character is revealed through a series of actions under stress, and the purpose of the story is reached at the moment of "epiphany," when the reader comes to know the true nature of a character or situation. Looked at from a distance and in light of the development of the short story, Salinger's stories are rather conventional. But when looked at from another way, the way suggested by the Zen *koan* that prefaces the collection, they become calligraphic paintings, reach their artistic high point in a tea ceremony, and have the arrangement of a Japanese garden.

Such a view of *Nine Stories* is not suggested as simply a critical metaphor or yet another way of getting at the problem of "pattern" that has bothered so many readers of the book. It is an acknowledgement that in these stories, Zen attitudes toward art and human experience are consciously being used by Salinger in dealing with and expressing such major themes as the survival of the despairing individual in a mass society, the redeeming possibilities in a lonely benevolent, intuitive kind of love, and the necessity of overcoming the pervasive obscenity of life by passing through the boundaries of personality to enlightenment, liberation, or *satori*. As Bernice and Sanford Goldstein have stressed in their study of the affinities between Salinger's work and Oriental thought, "Salinger's use of Zen and related Eastern experience . . . cannot be dismissed as pedantic and obtrusive, but emerges we believe as a driving force behind much of his writing. . . . Salinger's Zen is not that of a faddist or a dilettante."[1]

Salinger's interest in Zen began at least as early as the mid-1940s, and as we have seen, is important to the ending of *The Catcher in the Rye.* It might even be more crucial to the structure of the novel than we think. Holden's wanderings through the course of his story have been compared to those of Huckleberry Finn and Ulysses. And it even has been argued that the descent into the underworld in the *Aeneid* and into hell in the *Divine Comedy* provides a pattern for Holden's descent into his own private inferno. But why not suggest another famous quest as an archetype —that of the Buddha? The parallels are tempting.

The Buddha, whose family name was Gautama, lived in North India in the 6th century B. C. His story, like Holden's, begins at the age of sixteen when he has to confront the fact of adulthood. Here the stories seem to divide, because Gautama is married to a beautiful and devoted princess named Yasodhara and lives in a palace with every luxury at his command. But Holden's initiation into adulthood involves some of the same elements, although ironically presented. His sexual jealousy over Jane is a possessive one, the kind of jealousy that subconsciously, at least, makes marriage at once a necessary and, perhaps, impossible institution. Holden does not live in a palace, but his parents are fairly wealthy, he goes to an expensive school, and significant mention is made of the quality of his possessions, especially his luggage. Both Holden and Gautama thus find themselves in roughly similar situations, and both are compelled to set out on journeys.

Like Holden, Gautama is suddenly confronted with the reality of life and the suffering of mankind, and he decides to find the solution, a way out of universal suffering. After the birth of his only child, he leaves his kingdom and becomes an ascetic (notice that several times Holden emphasizes he seldom eats very much) in search of an answer. For six years Gautama wanders up and down the valley of the Ganges (Holden wanders up and down Manhattan), seeking out famous religious teachers, studying their systems and methods, and submitting himself to the most extreme self-denial. None of this satisfies him. Finally, after seven years of meditation in the forests, he sits down under the famous Bo-tree ("the Tree of Wisdom") on the bank of the river Neranjara, near Gaya in modern Bihar. During his time in the forest, he had struggled by the traditional means of contemplation and ascesis to penetrate the cause of man's enslavement to the manifold world of facts and events. All of his efforts had failed, and he was convinced that real understanding was not to be found. The more he concentrated, the more he found himself confused by his own concentration. At last, he simply gives up, goes off his rigid diet, and eats a good meal. At once he feels a change coming over him, and he sits beneath the tree, vowing that he would not rise until something more happened. He sits all night until his first glimpse of the morning star, and then he suddenly experiences a state of perfect clarity and understanding, an unexcelled complete awakening in which he feels liberated from the "Everlasting Round" of birth and death. What did he learn? Perhaps something like this: As long as a man tries to grasp at his own life, he is never free of the Round. Once he lets go, self-frustration is brought to an end, and it is this frustration (resulting from attempting the impossible, the desire for perfect control of the self and the environment) that is the cause of suffering.

From the Buddhist standpoint, the *actual* content of Gautama's experience could never be (and actually *was* never) put into words, and the experience of liberation retains its mysteries. It is a state to be obtained, but it cannot be sought; it occurs simultaneously after an act of resignation, but the resignation cannot occur until one has struggled to the point of resignation. A closer consideration of the Zen understanding of the experience in reference to *Nine Stories* will make these paradoxes more understandable, but for the moment let us consider the final scene with Holden and Phoebe at the park in *The Catcher in the Rye*. They have just left the zoo (Gautama's forest is full of animals). Holden *sits down* on a bench (no river, but it does start to rain), and as he watches Phoebe on the carousel (the "Everlasting Round" of birth and death), he experiences liberation. "My hunting hat really gave me a lot of protection, in a way, but I got soaked anyway," he says. "I didn't care, though. I felt so damn happy all of a sudden, the way old Phoebe kept going around and around" (p. 275). Gautama's moment of enlightenment came when he glimpsed the morning star, Holden's when he sees Phoebe, whose name is identified with the Roman goddess Diana, goddess of the moon. And like Gautama, Holden cannot and does not describe the experience in words. "I was damn near bawling," is all he can say, "I felt so damn happy, if you want to know the truth. I don't know why. It was just that she looked so damn *nice*, the way she kept going around and around, in her blue coat and all. God, I wish you could've been there" (p. 275). His hunting hat (a symbol of his quest, which has led him nowhere, has led to no solutions) is no real protection for him, of no real use to him as the rain starts to fall. But Holden just sits anyway, and as soon as he says he does not care, as soon as he lets go, he immediately feels happy.

Has Holden attained "Buddhahood" or awakening? Such an interpretation of the novel seems reasonable enough given the way Salinger indicates at the start of *Nine Stories* how that collection of fiction should be read—with a Zen *koan* in mind. *The Catcher in the Rye* and *Nine Stories* do not represent, after all, different phases of Salinger's life and work. The novel and the stories come roughly out of the same period; and from his treatment of Holden in "I'm Crazy" and "Slight Rebellion off Madison" in 1945 and 1946, we can assume that he was at least thinking about the novel while some of the stories were being written.

It is in *Nine Stories*, however, that Zen is most pointedly being used as a conceptualizing force for Salinger's fiction, and the puzzle that we are presented with before we can even start reading the stories is this one:

> We know the sound of two hands clapping.
> But what is the sound of one hand clapping?

This, of course, is one of the most famous Zen *koan*, originated by Hakuin (1685–1768), generally acknowledged as the greatest of the Zen masters. The word *Zen* means thinking, meditation, to see, to contemplate, and the *koan* is central to the Zen process. Zen is an anti-rational Buddhist sect that developed in India and that later became widespread in Japan; it differs from most of the other Buddhist sects in seeking enlightenment through introspection and intuition rather than in (Pali) scripture. Accordingly, Hakuin devised his famous *koan*, Heinrich Dumoulin explains in his *History of Zen Buddhism*, as "a problem which he believed would penetrate into one's consciousness with incomparable sharpness and would readily lead to the awakening of doubt and to progress in the exercises."[3] The "exercises," which are to a great extent the work of Hakuin, involve passing six series of tests involving five groups of *koan* and a sixth stage devoted to a study of the Buddhist precepts and the regulations of the monk's life as described in the light of Zen understanding. The *koan* Salinger cites is a preliminary *Hosshin* or first-level type, and its purpose is to profoundly acquaint the student with a way of thinking, a way of apprehending the nature of the self that is actually based on a theory of knowledge or what can be known.

Zen is the product of Oriental ways of thinking that do present some problems for the Western mind. This is because Westerners have generally taken what a Zen master would call a restricted view of human knowledge, what would be termed "conventional knowledge" or the assumption that we do not know anything unless we can put it in words or contain it within some systems of conventional signs (the notations of mathematics or music, for example). Conventional knowledge is a system of abstractions, consisting of signs and symbols in which things and events are reduced to their general outlines so that they can be comprehended one at a time. But we live in a universe that does not conform to this system, a universe in which things are happening altogether-at-once and whose reality escapes perfect definition through abstract terms. How then do we come to a better awareness of this "real" universe?

The Zen answer would be that we already know it without knowing it, and that what we call conscious, ordering thought is but a small function of our total consciousness. For instance, we have the notion of "controlling" our lives by adopting a role (doctor, carpenter, even priest), but life itself does not proceed in such a transparently artificial and cumbersome fashion. Our own organisms, for example, could not live for a minute if we had to take thought of every breath, every beat of the heart, every neural impulse. Yet we tend to hold to a conventional view of ourselves, even thinking about ourselves as a history consisting of selected memories, instead of the truer (in the Buddhist sense) realization that we each are simply what we are doing now.

This emphasis on coming to terms with the spon-

taneity of the self also suggests an idea of restoring our
original nature or returning to a state in which the
spontaneous rather than the conventional indeed
seemed most natural—to childhood. The peculiar nat-
uralness and un-self-consciousness of children is
gradually eliminated by conventional education
through which the child is taught not only what words
are to stand for what things, but also the way his
culture has arbitrarily agreed to divide things from
each other. The function of Zen is to undo the inevitable "damage" of this discipline, to encourage a state of
wholeness in which the mind functions freely and easily and spontaneously. The *koan* is the method by
which the Zen master "instructs" the student away
from conventional knowledge and reliance on wrong-
thinking.

The student begins with one assumption—that
the "Buddha nature" is within oneself and is not to be
sought outside. He does not have to journey to India
to find it. The master then asks the student a question,
presents him with a *koan*, and tells him to return when
he has discovered the answer, and to give some proof
of his discovery. In addition to the "one-hand" *koan*,
the "original face" *koan* is among the first to be presented, and perhaps makes for a better example of
what the stratagem involves. The "original face" *koan*
poses this question of the student: What was your
"original face," your basic nature, before your father
and mother conceived you? The student's first impulse
is to try to respond with philosophical and wordy answers. He may, using conventional reasoning, specu-
late on the origin of his *ego* and try to explain what is
meant by the term. But the master has no patience
with this—he wants to be "shown." The student then
might bring in "specimens of reality" such as a rock
and try to explain that before he was conceived he was
like the object, undesigned, without consciousness.

The master rejects all such approaches, and the student winds up at his wits' end, which is where he should be because he "knows that he does not know."

It is at this point that the mystery of Zen begins. The *koan* method is a process designed to produce *satori* or spontaneous comprehension of and communion with the true reality of self and nature and cannot be adequately described through words. It is, after all, a way of penetrating the fog of abstraction and therefore cannot be explained through further abstraction. But what happens is something like this— the student at last reaches the point of feeling utterly stupid. The metaphor that is often used in reference to this state is that of a huge block of ice in which the student is unable to move or think. He knows absolutely nothing; everything is as incomprehensible as "the sound of one hand." But then, after an undetermined time, there comes a moment when the ice suddenly melts. The problem of who he is becomes absurd; from the beginning, the question meant nothing. The knot has vanished because the abstraction of the mind seeking to know the mind has been defeated— no longer exists. When the student has reached this stage of liberation, the master knows that his training can now begin because it has (Zen relishes paradoxes) been finished.

The student, through continued practice, has an unobstructed mind into which the subsequent *koan* descend and are "solved" ("realized" might be a better word, although it too is inadequate). As the student finishes with each *koan*, the master usually requires that he present a verse from the *Zenrin Kushu*, an anthology of some five-thousand two-line poems, compiled by Toyo Eicho (1429–1504), or from some other book which expresses the point of the *koan* just solved. This is a practice that brings us directly back to *Nine Stories*, for each of the stories can be seen as a "verse" serving to comment on the *koan* with which the book begins. And just as the Zen "work" for the student involves alternating a crucial *koan* with subsidiary ones that explore the implications of the former, each story presents puzzles of its own that give us a working acquaintance with the Buddhist view of the universe.

What then is the point of the "one-hand" *koan*? It leads us through a series of questions. Can you hear something that is not making any noise? Can you get any sound out of a hand that has nothing to hit against? Can you obtain any knowledge of your own real nature—can the mind hit against itself? It is this final question that Salinger comes down to in his stories as he presents characters who achieve or fail to achieve *satori*, who either do or do not achieve a sudden and intuitive way of seeing into themselves. And for those who do solve the *koan* that is crucial to their awakening, what happens is described by Dumoulin this way: "He who lifts one hand and while listening quietly can hear a sound which no ears hear, can surpass all conscious knowledge. He can leave the world of distinctions behind him; he may cross the ocean of the *karma* of rebirths, and he may break through the darkness of ignorance. In the enlightenment he attains to unlimited freedom."[4]

To the western mind, this unlimited freedom is most easily symbolized in children, and this, of course, is why Salinger relies on the child as symbol so often in *Nine Stories*. Sybil of "A Perfect Day for Bananafish," Ramona of "Uncle Wiggily in Connecticut," Esmé in "For Esmé—With Love and Squalor," and even the outrageously precocious "Teddy" of the story bearing his name all embody, to one degree or another, the state of enlightenment against which Salinger posits the inadequate conventional wisdom of the adults who populate their world. To become like children, his adult characters must struggle with the *koan* paradox until their minds are literally dragged to the edge of Holden Caulfield's "crazy cliff" and beyond. The same thing happens to us as we read Salinger. His stories often end in a puzzling way, often with lines that at first seem to make no sense and we are forced to ask what happened, what does this mean. As we try to answer such questions, we find ourselves in the same dilemma as the student of Zen and come to realize that we are dealing with a stern taskmaster who is trying to guide us toward the Way, who is trying to get us to vomit up the apple of logic.

Appropriate to the Zen process, Salinger begins *Nine Stories* with what has long been seen as the most enigmatic and perplexing story in the collection, "A Perfect Day for Bananafish." The story opens with a woman sitting in a Miami Beach hotel room putting lacquer on her nails, reading an article ("Sex is Fun— or Hell") in a woman's pocket-size magazine, and waiting for a phone call from her mother in New York. When the call eventually comes through, we learn that the woman's husband, Seymour Glass, has a number of behavioral problems (he has crashed a car into a tree, he has a habit of deliberately insulting people), and that his mother-in-law has doubts about her daughter's sanity in even staying with him. The scene shifts to the beach where Seymour is talking to a ten-year-old child, Sybil Carpenter, who possesses the spontaneity Salinger carefully develops and represents in most of his child characters. Seymour and Sybil carry on a playful question-and-answer conversation that suggests the wise nonsense that is often a part of the Zen master-student relationship, and then he takes her into the water to look for a "bananafish," which Seymour describes this way: "they swim into a hole where there's a lot of bananas. They're very ordinary-

looking fish when they swim *in*. But once they get in,
they behave like pigs. Why, I've known some bananafish to swim into a banana hole and eat as many as
seventy-eight bananas. Naturally, after that they're so
fat that they can't get out of the hole again. Can't get
through the door" (p. 16).[5] They then die from
"banana fever." After listening to Seymour's little al-
legory, Sybil quietly says she has just seen a bananafish. Seymour kisses the arch of her foot, and they
return to the shore and part. Seymour goes to his hotel
room, where his wife is sleeping, takes out an Ortgies
calibre 7.65 automatic pistol, sits down on the bed,
and shoots himself.

Two questions dominate any interpretation of the
story: What is a bananafish? And why does Seymour
shoot himself? The latter question is particularly
troublesome, because in the subsequent books, *Franny
and Zooey* and *Raise High the Roof Beam, Carpenters; and Seymour: An Introduction*, Seymour becomes something of a saint. How can he be a saint if
he commits suicide? And are we expected to admire a
character who seems jaded, schizophrenic, precious,
and who might even have pedophiliac tendencies?

The critical responses to these questions have not
been consistent or satisfactory. The general agreement
is that the bananafish have something to do with the
satiation of the senses. The sea represents the blue
world of spirituality in which we may swim freely if
we only choose to do so. But most of us are bananafish
who prefer to swim into some dark place and become
such gluttons for sensual pleasure that we cannot swim
out again and are trapped. So, one interpretation is
William Wiegand's, that "Seymour, a bananafish himself, has become so glutted with sensation that he cannot swim out into society again. It is his own banana
fever, not his wife who is at fault, or his mother-in-

law."[6] But how can Salinger expect us to accept Seymour's eventual canonization if Seymour is himself trapped by what he denounces? One response has been to argue that the Seymour of "A Perfect Day for Bananafish" is not the same Seymour who figures so prominently in the Glass family dialogues, just as the Holden Caulfield of the early stories is not quite the same one who appears in *The Catcher in the Rye*. Since Seymour's suicide is fully acknowledged when he is later mentioned by his family, however, it is more likely that we must accept the Seymour Salinger gives us from the start. Such a choice has forced critics to adopt extreme positions, even going so far to suggest, as Kenneth Hamilton does, that Seymour's "suicide is his way of allowing the true Muriel to escape from the banana hole where she has become trapped through her attitude to marriage. In other words, he dies physically in order that she may live again spiritually. . . . because his love for Muriel demands from him a unique and sacrificial spiritual effort. This interpretation may seem farfetched. . . ."[7] Indeed it does.

The main difficulty with "A Perfect Day for Bananafish" is that it seems to end in a vacuum, and to many readers the end is altogether unsatisfactory, bringing to mind the truism that is taught in every creative writing class—the easiest and cheapest way to end a story is to kill off your hero. But one thing is often forgotten in reading the story: It should be read with "one-hand clapping" in mind. The *koan* asks us to consider a hand clapping with nothing to clap against, and the point involves obtaining knowledge of one's own real nature. Salinger's story ends with a suicide that conceptually is like "one hand clapping" because there seems to be no motivation, nothing to set the act against (nor do we even *hear* the pistol shot). But the point we are invited to contemplate, just as if the story itself is a representation of the *koan*, is what Seymour learned about his own nature that makes the characterization Salinger gives him so significant.

Seymour's very name suggests the Zen theme of the enigma of self-discovery, a theme that is actually put into the form of a *koan* when Sybil first appears in the story. As her mother is putting sun-tan oil on Sybil's shoulders, Sybil keeps repeating the question, "Did you see more glass" (p. 10)? Seymour is trying to "see more," but the question is, just what can he see. As the discussion of the "original face" *koan* indicated, the complexities of the self grasping the self are enormous. And the complexities are equally great in the question posed by Sybil. The word *glass* has, of course, two main connotations—a glass you can see through and glass in the sense of a mirror that reflects your own image back at you. The image that is reflected is a false one; it is reversed, untrue, and unreal, and obsession with it is nothing more than vanity. In Zen, trying to understand oneself this way is as absurd as are the student's efforts at discovering his "original face." But the other sense of *glass* as a window is a different matter, because self-understanding can result from *seeing through* oneself. The function of the *koan* is to encourage this kind of thought, to lead the student to the point where the glass of illusion is shattered.

The conversation between Seymour and Sybil is directed toward getting Sybil to see something. Seymour first encourages her to see herself in an alternate way. He insists that her bathing suit is blue instead of yellow. The color imagery is important here, because blue is associated with spirituality (the heavens are blue, the madonna's cloak is traditionally blue in sacred art) and yellow is associated with various aspects of the physical or carnal (the color is the color of gold and the color of cowardice). As the questioning proceeds, yellow images become increasingly crucial.

Seymour and Sybil discuss the story of "Little Black Sambo" and the six tigers who run around the tree until they turn into butter. "I thought they'd never stop," Seymour says, "I never saw so many tigers" (p. 14). What Seymour is directing Sybil toward here is a consideration of the "Great Round" of existence, the wheel of life. In Buddhist thought, the emphasis is on escaping from the endless round of existence, or at least in not getting so frantically absorbed in it that, like the tigers, you melt into it. And where does Sybil live? In *Whirly Wood*, Connecticut, that's where.

When Seymour tells Sybil the parable of the bananafish, the color yellow figures the same way as it does in "Little Black Sambo." Like the tigers, the bananafish become trapped in their own mortality. One might ask, however, what else are they supposed to do. After all they *are* bananafish, and is it not the fate of bananafish to eat bananas? Man is mortal? Is it not simply the fate of man to become trapped in his own mortality? The answer to these questions, and perhaps the overall problem of the story as well, is that before the bananafish enters the hole, he is something else—at least he is free to swim the blue depths. The same is true of man in Buddhist thought. We have lost sight of what went before. We see only our images as bananafish without seeing through them to another more spontaneous indescribable self more in tune with the blue spirituality to which we have become blind.

Sybil, at least, is not blind. She says she sees a bananafish, and in its mouth are six bananas. Seymour suddenly picks up one of her feet and kisses the arch in blessing. She has *seen more*, and the course of instruction has finished. Like Seymour, she lives up to her name. Sybil is taken by most commentators on the story to mean *witch* (and Sybil is this in that she is *bewitching*), but the word also means *seer*, and this seems to be the meaning that is most appropriate. She has seen through the clear water, through the glass, and she has seen what a bananafish is.

The idea of the bananafish also should be understood in its relationship to a puzzling reference Seymour makes to T. S. Eliot's famous poem *The Waste Land*, which deals with a theme that runs through Salinger's writing as well, the apparent failure of Western civilization. When Sybil, out of jealousy, mentions Sharon Lipschutz, another little girl at the hotel to whom Seymour has been paying some attention, he says, "How that name comes up. Mixing memory and desire" (p. 13). Eliot opens his poem with lines that, on one level, set forth man's entrapment in the cycle of the seasons, in the cycle of life itself, ruled by memories, motivated by desire, an endless and tedious round. In condemning the sterile futility of modern life, Eliot nonetheless suggests that the way out, the way to salvation is open if we will but heed it. One of the most important sections of the poem on this point is Part III, "The Fire Sermon," the title of which is taken from the sermon the Buddha delivered in the Deer Park at Benares after he experienced his awakening. In this sermon (which corresponds in importance to Christ's Sermon on the Mount), the Buddha warns against surrender to the senses, which are on fire with passion, hatred, infatuation, birth, old age, death, sorrow, grief and despair. When the disciple becomes purged of passion, he becomes free and knows that rebirth is accomplished.

Eliot shows the disappointment that surrender to the senses brings by using the example of a "typist home at teatime" who sits in her one-room flat amid her beauty aids waiting for her lover. The typist is conceptually very similar to Salinger's depiction of Seymour's wife, Muriel, whose vapidity and sterility are suggested in the magazine article she is reading. Is sex fun—or hell? How would she know? It is also important to note, by way of parallel here, that when the typist's lover leaves, "She turns and looks a moment in the *glass*, / Hardly aware of her departed lover" (italics mine).[8] She does not see through the glass; she sees only her own vain reflection. Muriel suffers from the same kind of blindness; unlike Sybil, she can see only her own reflection as she tweezes out two freshly surfaced hairs in the mole on her face at the start of the story. And what will be her reaction to Seymour's suicide? Eliot's next two lines may suggest what Salinger has in mind: "Her brain allows one half-formed thought to pass: / 'Well now that's done: and I'm glad it's over.'"

But what about the suicide itself? *The Waste Land* develops around the archetype of death and resurrection; and an idea shared by Christianity, Buddhism, and other religions and practices that have a tradition of asceticism is that to live in the spirit one must die in the flesh. Seymour's suicide could thus be understood metaphorically, but this hardly seems satisfying. A better approach would be to go back to "The Fire Sermon" in which the Buddha set forth the "Four Noble Truths" that are essential to the purgation of the passions.

The first truth involves an inescapable fact of human life—suffering. Life as we usually live it is a matter of sorrow and grief. We are bound with things we dislike, and parted from things we like. And the more we try to grasp the world and ourselves, the more both change. The second truth relates to the cause of the suffering—mistaking the abstract world of things and occurrences for the concrete world of reality, and also making the mistake that one can grasp and control life. Such grasping leads to pure self-frustration and imprisonment in the vicious circle of birth and death. The third noble truth is concerned with the ending of self-frustration, an ending called *nirvana*.

This is a complicated term that is perhaps best understood through its Sanskrit etymology, in which it means the blowing out of a flame or the cessation of waves or circlings of the mind. Another way to understand it is as "de-spiration," the act of seeing the futility of trying to hold one's breath or life indefinitely, since to hold the breath is to lose it. *Nirvana* is thus release or liberation through "letting go"—to lose one's life is to find it. The fourth noble truth describes the method whereby self-frustration is brought to an end and *nirvana* is realized. The method is an "Eightfold Path" involving the attainment of complete view, complete understanding, complete (truthful) speech, complete action, complete vocation, complete application, complete recollectedness, and complete contemplation.

If the "Four Noble Truths" are applied to Seymour's life as an organizing principle, it is possible to argue that his suicide is symbolically related to *nirvana*. His flame is literally "blown away" and the circlings of his mind do come to an end, and he "lets go." He indicates in his discussion of "Little Black Sambo" and the parable of the bananafish that he is aware of the nature of suffering and its cause, and he seems to have completed the "Eightfold Path." What he must then attain is *nirvana*, meaning his disappearance from the Wheel of Life or the Round of incarnations into a state that escapes definition by being immeasurable and infinite. Reaching *nirvana* means awakening into Buddhahood. But this is not an *attainment*, because it cannot be sought directly. No acquisition and no motivation are involved in such an awakening, and the apparent lack of motivation in Seymour's suicide is thus tangentially justifiable.

Annihilation of the senses through suicide is, at any rate, in keeping with the characterization Salinger gives Seymour, and the very contemplation of why he commits suicide leads us, as a *koan* would, into the deeper consideration of the true reality of self and the world. It is also important to realize that suicide does not have the negative connotations in Buddhism that it does in Christianity. One only has to think of the Buddhist monks who immolated themselves with burning gasoline during the war in Viet Nam. Seymour's death takes on another aspect when we consider it as an act of protest, a protest against the phoniness embodied by Muriel and Miami Beach, the same kind of phoniness that so oppresses Holden Caulfield.

This is the phoniness that afflicts the heroine of the next story, "Uncle Wiggily in Connecticut," who lives in a suburb that could not be much different from Sybil's "Whirly Wood" in its symbolic association with the "Everlasting Round." And the house inside of which the story takes place on a darkening winter day is a direct reminder of Seymour's bananafish hole. This reiteration of ideas and images from story to story is, by the way, a technique that continues throughout the collection and serves to reinforce the *koan-* structure of the book.

Most of the story involves a conversation between two old college roommates, Eloise and Mary Jane, in Eloise's house as they sit drinking cocktails and talking about former acquaintances. Eloise's young daughter, Ramona, comes in, and the resentment Eloise feels toward her is disturbing. Ramona has problems with her eyes and wears thick glasses, yet she possesses imagination and spontaneity, and has invented an imaginary playmate, "Jimmy Jimmereeno," because there are no other children in the neighborhood. Here we have a continuation of the wasteland theme of the sterility of modern life. As sterile a person as Eloise is, her childless neighbors nonetheless call her "Fertile Fanny" behind her back.

After Ramona goes outside to play, Eloise begins to tell Mary Jane about Walt Glass, Seymour's brother and her lover during the war. She remembers him as superior to her husband, Lew, in every way. Walt had an odd and tender sense of humor, and once, when Eloise twisted her ankle, he called it "Poor Uncle Wiggily." Another time, when they were riding on a train, he placed his hand on her stomach and said it was "so beautiful he wished some officer would come up and order him to stick his other hand through a window" (p. 30). In saying this, Walt was expressing a *koan* of sorts, reflecting the Buddhist conception of the duality of opposites, that there are pleasures so great that the only way they can be comprehended is through contemplation of pain that would be equally great. But Eloise has never been able to solve the *koan*, nor has she been able to accept the absurdity of Walt's death—he was killed when a little Japanese stove he was packing for a colonel to send home as a souvenir blew up.

Like a bananafish, Eloise has retreated into suburbia, and as the afternoon wears on into evening, she and Mary Jane pour drink after drink. Ramona comes back in and tells them that Jimmy has been run over in the street, and Eloise sends her to bed. At seven o'clock, when the telephone rings, the room is dark and Eloise and Mary Jane are both nearly comatose. Eloise answers the call and cruelly tells her husband that she cannot come to the station to pick him up. She staggers upstairs to check on Ramona and is infuriated to see the girl sleeping way over on one side of the bed (she had a habit of doing that to leave room for Jimmy). Eloise screams at her, and Ramona explains that she has a new friend, "Mickey Mickeranno." Eloise loses her temper and forces Ramona to sleep in the middle of the bed. But then, suddenly full of remorse and without obvious motivation, she picks up

Ramona's glasses and begins to cry as she says "Poor Uncle Wiggily" over and over again. Finally she puts the glasses back on the table, lenses down, and kisses Ramona.

Like so many other Salinger characters, she is led by the example of a child to suddenly see through her life and come to a better understanding of her true nature. And again, *glass* figures prominently as a symbol. She had spent the afternoon and much of her life drinking from glasses without realizing that suffering cannot be escaped through satiation. But it is not until she sees through the glasses of a child that she begins to "see more."

Not only does she realize that in marrying Lew after the death of Walt she was trying to "re-invent" a replacement for her dead lover just as casually as Ramona replaces Jimmy Jimmereeno with Mickey Mickeranno; she also is led toward the cure for banana fever in realizing that she has not always been the way she is now, so terribly trapped in the circumstances that surround her. She goes back downstairs, wakes up Mary Jane, and asks her, "I was a nice girl, wasn't I" (p. 38)? The question is a plea and it is a pathetic one full of a foolish longing for lost innocence and delivered on a vodka breath, but it is a plea in the form of a *koan*. It is a short step from "nice girl" to "original face," and the story ends movingly and hopefully. We do not know what Eloise is going to do about her phony life with Lew, but we know now that she is going to do something. "She is," as Warren French carefully explains, "like a character in Dante's Inferno who cannot escape but who has just discovered where he really is."[9]

Eloise's discovery is prompted by her picking up Ramona's glasses, and it is just by such signs or signals that moments of awakening are triggered in many of Salinger's stories. It is in the tradition of Zen that the

real message always remains unspoken and that what
cannot be conveyed by speech can nevertheless be
communicated by "direct pointing," without which the
Buddhist experience, because of the essential mysticism behind it, could never have been passed from
generation to generation. Zen even maintains (by way
of illustration on this matter of the importance of signs
and gestures) that the Buddha transmitted the meaning of awakening to his chief disciple by holding up a
flower and saying nothing. We can see Salinger's use
of a similar device in one of his most muted stories,
"Just Before the War with the Eskimos," in which the
sign is not a pair of glasses; it is half of a chicken
sandwich.

     Ginnie Mannox, who is five-foot-nine, wears size 9-
B shoes, and is awkwardly uncertain of herself, is
angry with her fellow classmate and tennis partner,
Selena Graff, because Selena never volunteers to pay
her half of the cab fare after their Saturday morning
tennis sessions. Ginnie insists on following Selena into
her apartment to collect the $1.90 she insists Selena
owes her. While she is waiting for Selena to get the
money from her mother, Selena's brother, Franklin,
comes in. He is dishevelled and repulsive looking, and
complains about cutting his finger on some razorblades
while reaching into a wastepaper basket. While he is
talking to Ginnie, he picks food from between his
teeth with a fingernail and scratches off scabs. He is a
bananafish of a different type, so immersed in the
Round of pain and suffering that his very agony begins
to fascinate Ginnie, and she begins to ask questions
that probe the sources of his anguish. She learns that
he had met her sister, Joan, whom he calls a snob, at a
party in 1942, and that he had written her eight letters
and never received an answer. She learns that he has a
bad heart and that he had to spend the war years
working in an airplane factory. And when Franklin's

friend, Eric, comes to pick him up, she learns that Franklin is a homosexual.

But at one moment in the story, Franklin, with all of his bitterness and sarcasm, is suddenly moved by one of those instances of lonely benevolence and concern that come up here and there in Salinger's fiction. He sits holding his bleeding finger and says, "I don't like it when it stings." Ginnie simply tells him to stop touching it, and at once Franklin responds as if he has experienced an awakening. "As though responding to an electric shock," Salinger writes, "Selena's brother pulled back his uninjured hand. He sat up a trifle straighter—or rather, slumped a trifle less. He looked at some object on the other side of the room. An almost dreamy expression came over his disorderly features" (p. 45). A basic point in Buddhism is one contained in the "Four Noble Truths," that suffering is, in a sense, its own cause. It is this that Franklin suddenly understands as he sees through himself, sees through his own agony, and stops "touching it."

He is so moved that he insists Ginnie accept a gift, half of a chicken sandwich he has kept in his room. He insists that she take a bite of it. And when she does, she nearly gags because of his repulsive appearance and manners, but she manages to swallow a small part of the sandwich. The sandwich takes on a sacramental quality and suggests the underlying fable of incarnation—the revelation of spirit through matter —that runs through this story and most of the others in *Nine Stories*. Just as she is forced to take a bite of the sandwich, she is forced to get a taste of what Franklin's life is like and, in turn, better understand her own. She also sees through herself, senses the phoniness in her own life, realizes that her sister is indeed a snob and that she could end up the same way, and that perhaps she has been too self-centered in her relationship with Selena. She refuses to accept

the money when Selena returns with it, and even suggests that the two of them do something that night as
friends.

The title of the story underscores the extent of
liberation with which it ends. Both Ginnie and Franklin are caught in an endless round of things—she in
her pettiness, he in his awareness of his own suffering
and his tendency to feel sorry for himself. He is in
such despair over the absurdity of human existence,
that he sees no end to the continuing cycle of mortal
foolishness. One war has ended, but people are running to the draft boards to sign up for another. Franklin sarcastically prophesies that the next war will
probably be against the Eskimos. Life is that absurd.
But through their contact with each other, the essential absurdity has been seen through. "Salinger has
struck his note," Josephine Jacobsen writes. "The sor-
did, soulless, hopeless, pointless has been fractured by
the force of the delicate, irresistible infusion: the
human exchange of beatific signals."[10]

The exchange does not always work so smoothly,
however, and the process of awakening is sometimes a
chilly one involving revelations that can seem like
punishment at the moment they occur. This is what is
discovered by the narrator of "The Laughing Man," a
story about the destruction of the spontaneous, irrational, and imaginative world of childhood.

The narrator takes us back to 1928 when he was
nine and a member of the Comanche Club, whose
leader was a law student at N. Y. U. named John
Gedsudski (referred to by his young charges as the
"Chief"), a former Eagle Scout, nearly an All-America
tackle in 1926, and he had even been invited to try out
with the New York Giants baseball team. But the
Chief's most memorable ability is as a storyteller. At
the end of each outing, after the boys had finished
playing soccer or football or baseball, the Chief would

straddle the driver's seat in the bus and continue the fantastic adventures of The Laughing Man, who was kidnapped by Chinese bandits as a child. His missionary parents refused to pay his ransom, and the bandits squeezed his head in a vise, leaving him with hideous features (no nose, an enormous oval cavity for a mouth). The bandits let him stay with them, however, but only if he keeps his face covered with a red mask of poppy petals. The Laughing Man soon develops the resourcefulness of the outcast, and daily goes into the forest where he befriends animals. Meanwhile, he picks up on the bandits' trade secrets and becomes more successful at banditry than they are, and they try to kill him. He succeeds in locking them up in a mausoleum (they escape every now and then and he has to round them up each time), and expands his operations by crossing the border from China into France. Despite his mortal enemy, the detective Marcel Dufarge, the Laughing Man acquires the largest fortune in the world. He gives most of his money to a monastery, and converts the rest to diamonds and lowers it in vaults into the Black Sea. His own needs are simple—he lives on rice and eagle's blood. And not even his closest companions, a timber wolf named Black Wing, the lovable dwarf Omba, the giant Mongolian Hong, and a beautiful Eurasian girl, had ever seen his face.

What the Laughing Man represented to the narrator was more than simply a fantasy figure. The Laughing Man provided him with an objective correlative of his own "original face," the perception of the self beyond the self that is more possible in the Zen-world of children than it is in the conventional world of adulthood. "I was not even my parents' son in 1928," he tells us, "but a devilishly smooth imposter, awaiting their slightest blunder as an excuse to move in—preferably without violence, but not necessarily—

to assert my true identity. . . . But the *main* thing I had
to do in 1928 was watch my step. Play along with the
farce. Brush my teeth. Comb my hair. At all costs,
stifle my natural hideous laughter" (pp. 61–62). It is
the true identity, the natural laughter that the Zen
experience is supposed to lead to—the very things the
rational adult world inevitably suppresses as the child
grows up and is forced to "play along with the farce."

The members of the Comanche Club sense that a
change is about to occur when the picture of a girl
appears on the visor of the bus one day. The picture is
of Mary Hudson, the Chief's girlfriend and a graduate
of Wellesley, who even has the nerve a few days later
to board the bus herself, ride to the park with the
boys, and join in their baseball game. Their resentment at this female intrusion soon dissolves, however,
when they discover what a good baseball player she is.
She is so good and such a good sport that the narrator
develops a crush on her, and for a while the Comanche Club becomes a wonderful extended family.

But one day in April, the Chief shows up wearing
an overcoat and has his hair combed. He stops where
he usually picks up Mary and, to kill some time, begins
an installment of the Laughing Man that ends with
Dufarge firing a full clip of his automatic at the
Laughing Man point blank. Then the Chief gives up
waiting for Mary and drives to the park. In the third
or fourth inning of the game, the narrator spots Mary
sitting on a bench a hundred yards away. The Chief
goes to her, talks to her, and the two of them return to
the field. Mary sits down on another bench and refuses
to play. In his confusion over what is happening, the
narrator asks what is wrong; she asks to be left alone,
and at the end of the game she runs away from the
Chief crying.

When the boys get back on the bus, the Chief

finishes the story. As the bullets are fired, the Laughing Man contracts his stomach muscles, catches the slugs, and expels them. Dufarge drops dead in shock, but the Laughing Man is still in trouble; he is lashed to a tree with barbed wire. He falls back on one of his last resources, calls the animals to him, and sends them for help. Omba eventually finds him and reveals that the Dufarges have killed his beloved Black Wing. In despair, the Laughing Man dies. His last act is to pull off the mask.

We never learn for sure what went wrong between the Chief and Mary, but part of the tension between them results from the artificial distinctions of social class. His name suggests his ethnic-minority status, and her name of Hudson indicates that she may come from an old-line American family. He lives in Staten Island, and she lives in fashionable Douglaston, Long Island. Even their appearances suggest their differences—he is short and stocky, with a large nose and a low hairline; she is beautiful. But the final conflict between them may involve more than their differences in social status; it may be that the Chief has made Mary pregnant, something the narrator could be alluding to when, during the game, she tells him to leave her alone and he begins to walk backward to his position on the field: "It was the kind of whole certainty, however independent of the sum of its facts, that can make walking backwards more than normally hazardous, and I bumped smack into a baby carriage" (p. 70). The baby carriage is another one of Salinger's signs, and it points toward a kind of negative illumination for the narrator. Whatever has happened between the Chief and Mary, the irrational, wonderfully spontaneous world of the Laughing Man cannot be allowed to go on, and when the narrator gets off the bus, he sees a piece of red tissue paper flapping in the wind at the base of a lamppost. "I arrived home with my teeth chattering uncontrollably," he says, "and was told to go right straight to bed" (p. 73).

The negative initiation of the narrator into the restrictions and rational cruelties of adulthood is painfully detailed in the story, but our sympathetic interest gradually becomes focused on the Chief, who is, like some of Salinger's earlier characters, at the stage in his life where the meaning of his existence is a central question. But his movement is away from enlightenment, and at the end he has given up trying to hear the sound of "one hand clapping." When he strips away the Laughing Man's mask he destroys his own belief in the value of irrational exuberance, and the nature he reveals is indeed a hideous one.

What the story of the Laughing Man represents is the Chief's attempt at trying to discover his own "original face" through imagination, through coming up with a fictional approximation of the *koan* that is behind it. But because of circumstance, perhaps because of his own immersion in the conventional world (he is, after all, a *law* student), perhaps because he is trying too hard, he achieves the opposite of liberation: negation. The *koan* exercise is not a simple process, and it can lead to disaster. "The unnatural suppression of reason is a gamble," Dumoulin cautions. "It may destroy the psychic structure of a person permanently and irremediably."[11] "The Laughing Man" is one of the bleakest and disturbing stories in the collection, and it cautions that the way of Zen is not easy.

But the story is a delightful one. It shows Salinger's imagination at its best as the episodic adventures of the Laughing Man are elaborated, and the peculiar world of childhood as contained within the Comanche Club is vividly poignant. As a tale of initiation, it certainly ranks with Sherwood Anderson's "I Want to Know Why," and in it sheer relish of recollection evokes the best of Jean Shepherd—all of which serves, among other things, to diminish the next story by comparison.

In many ways, "Down at the Dinghy" is the slightest piece in the collection. It does move toward a moment of enlightenment and it does include another of Salinger's precociously symbolic children, but it ultimately turns on a revelation that, at worst, makes it seem forced and, at its best, precious. The story begins with Sandra, the maid, and Mrs. Snell, the ironing lady, sitting at the kitchen table at the Tannenbaum's vacation house talking about the behavior of their employers' four-year-old son who has the habit of running away, which he has been doing at intervals since he was two. The lady of the house, Boo Boo, a sister of Seymour Glass, comes into the kitchen to get a pickle so she can lure her son out of the dinghy that is tied to the end of the dock. He is sitting at the tiller in the stern of the boat pretending to sail away. She tries to get him to tell her why he wants to leave this time, and finally, after a child-adult conversation that, as they occasionally do in Salinger, becomes cloying, she learns the reason. He tells his mother that he had overheard Sandra tell Mrs. Snell that his father is a "big— sloppy—kike." Boo Boo takes him in her arms and then gently asks him if he knows what the word means. "It's one of those things that go up in the *air*," he says. "With *string* you hold" (p. 86). Boo Boo is immensely touched by his innocence and spontaneity as she sees how absurd the problems of the obscene adult world are when viewed through the mind of the child. But the first reaction is perhaps to agree with Maxwell Geismar, that it is "a tricky little bit of anti-anti Semitism,"[12] even though the Zen idea comes through—that intuitive and loving intelligence is an effective weapon against an obtuse world that prefers vicious labels instead of enlightened vision (at one point in his anger and confusion, the boy throws his uncle Seymour's swimming goggles overboard).

If "Down at the Dinghy" is the low point in the book, "For Esmé—With Love and Squalor" is just the opposite. Like "The Laughing Man," the story is narrated in the first person and takes the form of recollection. The narrator has received an invitation to a wedding in England, and though he decides he cannot attend, he tells us that he will jot down a few notes on the bride as he knew her six years ago. "Nobody's aiming to please here," he states as his aesthetic at the start. "More, really, to edify, to instruct" (p. 87). And that is what the story turns out to be—one of the most edifying in the book, but also one of the most pleasing as well.

In April 1944, the narrator was taking a British Intelligence course at Devon in England. On the last day of the three-week term of instruction, he decides to walk from the barracks through the rain into town. He sees a notice for children's choir practice on a church bulletin board and goes inside, where he sits listening to the children singing, paying special attention to a thirteen-year-old girl with an exquisite face. He leaves the church and seeks shelter from the rain in a tearoom. A few minutes after he sits down, the girl from the choir enters with her young brother and their governess, and the girl asks if she might join him. She tells him about herself in a strained, slightly pompous, and pseudo-sophisticated manner that is nonetheless full of effervescence, naiveté, and sheer youthfulness. Both of her parents are dead, she explains, and she lives with her aunt. Her father was killed in a battle in Africa, and she is wearing the chronographic watch that had belonged to him. She learns that the narrator is a writer, and she asks him if he will write a story for her—one with lots of "squalor" in it, a word she does not define, indeed cannot define because of her innocence. After asking him if she can send letters to him, she leaves.

The second part of the story, one in which the full contrast between the world of Esmé and the world of the sergeant is presented, provides plenty of squalor. The recollection is so painful, that the narrator has chosen to refer to himself in the third person, as "Sergeant X."[13] The story shifts to Bavaria where Sergeant X is stationed after being hospitalized for a nervous breakdown. He is far from recovered and feels "rather like a Christmas tree whose lights, wired in series, must all go out if even one bulb is defective" (p. 106). He is not suffering from battle fatigue so much as he is from the same thing as Holden Caulfield—the utter obscenity of life. When his jeep partner, Corporal Clay, comes in and tells him how the corporal's girl friend's psychology class discussed and interpreted a battle incident involving the shooting of a cat, Sergeant X throws up. After Clay leaves, the Sergeant thinks of trying to steady himself by composing a letter to a friend in New York, but his hands are shaking so badly he cannot get the paper into the typewriter. Then he notices an unopened package on his desk. Inside, he finds a note from Esmé along with her father's wristwatch, which she wants him to have because it is "extremely water-proof and shockproof as well as having many other virtues among which one can tell at what velocity one is walking if one wishes" (p. 113). He sits with the watch in his hand, and then he feels wonderfully calm and "ecstatically" sleepy.

The story thus ends with a moment of liberation in which the human exchange of beatific signals (again involving the interaction of a child and an adult) has taken place. The crystal of the watch is broken, it may no longer be waterproof, and quite likely it will not be able to tell the Sergeant how fast he is going. But all of that does not matter; it is what the watch points to in the Zen sense that is important. It is the signal (like the Buddha's flower) that prompts his awakening. The crystal, of course, brings to mind the *glass* that has to be broken, has to be penetrated and seen through. The water that may leak through the crystal is a universal symbol of cleansing and rebirth. And the Sergeant does not need to know how fast he is going, because he has gotten to where he has to be in the truest Zen fashion—by sitting.

Appropriately enough for a story with such an ending, "For Esmé—With Love and Squalor" has a *koan* at its center. While the Sergeant and Esmé are talking in the tearoom, her little brother Charles keeps interrupting to ask a riddle, "What did one wall say to the other wall?" The first time Charles asks it, the Sergeant lets him provide his own answer, "Meetcha at the corner." But the second time Charles asks the same question, the Sergeant answers it for him, and Charles stalks away in anger. Charles, with the spontaneous mind of the child, can answer the *koan*. It does not work, indeed it is utterly wrong, for an adult like the Sergeant to answer the riddle simply because he has been *told* the answer. He has to work it out for himself, and then it can be expressed only indirectly through citing a verse from scripture or a passage from literature that complements its meaning.

As Esmé and Charles leave, the Sergeant does pass into the world of squalor as he contemplates Charles's *koan*. What might one wall say to another? The wall is a symbol for a dead end and also suggests isolation. What *could* one wall say to another? While sitting in his room, which is in a house that had been occupied by a Bavarian family a few weeks before, the Sergeant picks up a book that had belonged to a daughter of the family. It is a book by Joseph Goebbels, the Nazi war propagandist, entitled *Die Zeit Ohne Beispiel* (*Unparallelled Times*). The daughter had written the words, "Dear God, life is hell," on the flyleaf. This is what one wall might say to another, but it is a statement that, however true it might be for its author, is only another form of propaganda to the Zen thinker. "Nothing led up to or away from it," the narrator states. "Alone on the page, and in the sickly stillness of the room, the words appeared to have the stature of an uncontestable, even classic indictment" (p. 105). The Sergeant stares at the page, and then writes down an inscription from Dostoevsky "Fathers and teachers, I ponder 'What is hell?' I maintain that it is the suffering of being unable to love." When the Sergeant looks over what he has written, he discovers, to his horror, that it was almost entirely illegible. Pondering such abstractions as *hell* and *love* get him nowhere.

But when he opens Esmé's package and contemplates the watch, the beatific signal she has sent him, the answer to the riddle suddenly manifests itself. It is the same one Charles had provided, "Meetcha at the corner," but it was not the correct one for the Sergeant until it came to him in an awakening. What happens to two walls when they meet at the corner? They lose themselves in each other and see through the problem of selfhood. When does a wall stop being a wall and become a corner? When does the isolated, flat-surfaced, superficial self transcend itself? It is through moments such as those the Sergeant experiences. He meets Esmé at the corner before he goes around the bend.

Salinger's confidence in the redeeming powers of the kind of love that is expressed through the lonely benevolence of Esmé is at its peak in this story and falls off drastically in "Pretty Mouth and Green My Eyes," a story that disintegrates into pathos and, uncharacteristically, is without any healing sympathy. It does function within the collection much like "The

Laughing Man," however, because it presents the dangerous side of the Zen experience through characters who do not work their way through life's essential *koan*. And the story serves as a near-perfect counterpoint to "For Esmé—with Love and Squalor" because it features three characters who are literally up against their individual walls and who will never meet at the corner.

Critics have often commented on the use Salinger makes of telephone conversations in expressing the difficulty his characters have in talking directly to one another face-to-face. "Pretty Mouth and Green My Eyes" carries this device to an extreme, because the story consists almost entirely of a telephone conversation late at night between an older lawyer and a younger man in the same firm. The young man, Arthur, is concerned about what has happened to his wife. She did not come home with him after a party and he wonders where she is. The older man, Lee, tries to offer him advice and comfort, and encourages him to have a nightcap and go to bed. But all the while Lee is trying to comfort Arthur, he is in bed with Arthur's wife. A story so heavily loaded with irony could not possibly succeed, and this one is no exception. It ends with Arthur trying to save face by telling Lee that the wife, Joanie, has just walked in.

But what "Pretty Mouth and Green My Eyes" lacks in transcendence is made up for by "De Daumier-Smith's Blue Period," a story that, like some of Salinger's other better ones, features a first-person narrator who recollects a traumatic period in his life that ends with the most vivid account of the Zen experience we find anywhere in Salinger. Unfortunately, the rest of the story does not quite justify its conclusion.

On one level, the story reads as if it is a treatment of the classic Oedipal situation, the narrator recounting how he returned to New York from Paris in the company of his stepfather after the death of his mother, both of them discovering that their only bond is that they are both in love with the same dead woman. And to a certain extent, the story does deal with the hero's movement toward sexual and psychological maturation, but this is only a consequence of his experiencing an awakening of a profounder sort that leads to a sacramental view of life and an understanding of his "original face."

After studying art for a time in New York, the narrator writes a letter of application for a job at an academy in Montreal, "Les Amis Des Vieux Maitres." In the letter, he assumes the name used in the story's title, and he also fills the letter with lies about himself, his past, and his qualifications. The school, which is located above an orthopedic appliance shop, turns out to be a correspondence school run by M. Yoshoto, a Japanese artist, whose most memorable work is a beautifully simple watercolor that is a perfect example of Zen painting, "a certain white goose flying through an extremely pale-blue sky . . .—the blueness of the sky, or an ethos of the blueness of the sky, reflected on the bird's feathers" (p. 140). The color imagery here suggests what must happen to Daumier-Smith, that he must overcome the "blues" brought on by his own self-deception and phoniness and exchange them for the blueness of the sky, the ethos of which is a mystic vision of spirituality. But this is not so easily accomplished.

Daumier-Smith's ideas on life and art are so confused, he so loathes other people, and he feels so sorry for himself that his condition seems hopeless in its horrible isolation. As he confesses, "everything I touched turned to solid loneliness" (p. 132). At first, the students he is assigned do nothing but depress him with either their ineptness or their ability to relish obscenity. One is a twenty-three-year old Toronto housewife named Bambi Kramer who did wretchedly executed drawings with such titles as "Forgive Them Their Trespasses" (showing small boys fishing by a "No Fishing" sign). Another is a society photographer named R. Howard Ridgefield who liked to paint pictures of chaste young girls with udder-sized breasts being assaulted in church by the minister, the shadow of the altar in the background. And some of his other students are even worse. But one, a nun of the order of Sisters of St. Joseph named Sister Irma, moves him strangely because of her very egolessness.

She has enclosed no photograph in her application papers, does not reveal her age, and leaves all of her work unsigned, and in doing this she unwittingly becomes a *sign* to him, in her very Zen-like simplicity a beatific signal. Daumier-Smith writes a letter to her that is the first honest and thoughtful communication he has ever had with anyone, and it is apparent that he has fallen in love with her. He even asks what her visiting hours at the convent are, and has a fantasy that perhaps she has not taken her final vows and is free to run away with him. His fantasy is abruptly ended, however, when a letter returns from the Mother Superior of Sister Irma's convent saying that the nun would not be allowed to continue her study at Les Amis Des Vieux Maitres.

The letter is especially shattering to the narrator because the evening before he receives it, he experiences a realization about himself that is overwhelmingly distressing. On his way back to his room after a night out, he stops on the sidewalk and looks into the display window of the orthopedic appliances shop. "Then something altogether hideous happened," he recalls. "The thought was forced on me that no matter how coolly or sensibly or gracefully I might one day learn to live my life, I would at best be a visitor in a garden of enamel urinals and bedpans, with a sightless, wooden dummy-deity standing by in a marked-down rupture truss" (p. 157). It is this vision of life, his conception of the nature of human suffering and the horrible frustration of trying to control things, that prepares him for the "letting go" that must precede awakening.

After he reads the letter concerning Sister Irma's withdrawal from the school, he goes up to his room, sits down on a cushion, and stares at a hole in the window blind. Then he gets up and writes a second letter to Irma, one he never mails because "The substance seemed . . . a trifle thin" (p. 162). Later he gets dressed up and goes out intending to get drunk. But at nine o'clock, he finds himself in front of the display window again. A woman shop assistant is in the window putting a new truss on a dummy. She is so startled at finding herself observed that she steps back on a stack of irrigation basins and falls down. Daumier-Smith reaches out to prevent her fall only to hit his fingertips on the glass. Suddenly he experiences a flash of insight. The sun appears to come up and speeds toward the bridge of his nose at the speed of light. He is blinded and frightened and has to put his hand on the window to keep his balance. When his sight returns, the girl is gone, "leaving behind her a shimmering field of exquisite, twice-blessed, enamel flowers" (p. 164). As he reaches out to help the girl, he is made powerfully aware of his own isolation and ineffectuality. But the very impulse, his desire to reach out through the invisible wall that separates them, enables him to experience self-transcendence and the ugliness of man's mortal nature at its worst (the obscenity of the urinals and bedpans *on display*) turns into beauty.

What is it he has realized? Again, it cannot be stated directly, but he gives us an approximation when he goes to his room and writes, some hours later, that he is "giving Sister Irma her freedom to follow her own destiny. Everybody is a nun" (p. 164). What this *koan* (Why is everybody a nun?) suggests is that being human means being devoted to a religious life, and that everyone must try to discover the path of spiritual awareness, an awareness that can come in a blinding illumination only when the point of "letting go" is reached. The story does not end with the awakening, however. We see its continuing influence on Daumier-Smith. He stops being a phony, he has increased sympathy for others, and even though he returns to his stepfather after the school fails, his Oedipal difficulties have disappeared. He is even able to happily devote himself to the wonderfully well-adjusted pursuit of "the American Girl in Shorts" (p. 165).

We are left at the end, however, with the feeling that this story is a little too much of an exercise in Buddhist psychotherapy. Daumier-Smith gets straightened-out too fast and too thoroughly, and the problem may be in the lack of secondary characterization. The step-father, to whom the story is dedicated, scarcely figures in it. M. Yoshoto remains just what a Japanese character should not be in a good piece of fiction—inscrutable. And Sister Irma's self-effacement is so complete that Daumier-Smith's overwhelming response to her work is a little hard to accept as anything other than blind and unexpected enthusiasm. But the main weakness in the story could be that, as Paul Kirschner suggests, "for the first time Salinger seems to depend on religious response in his reader instead of working to create one."[14]

This is a reaction that carries over into the collection's last story, "Teddy," which features as its protagonist a child who is so precocious that his parents have taken him to England where he has been examined at Oxford and Edinburgh by some of the world's leading savants. Teddy, his parents, and his emotion-

ally disturbed six-year-old sister (she hates everybody) are on an ocean liner returning to the United
States as the story opens. The action, as such, consists
almost entirely of a dialogue between Teddy and a
young professor of education, Bob Nicholson. Through
this conversation, we learn that Teddy is a believer in
the Vedantic theory of reincarnation, that he was a
holy man in India in his last incarnation, that he almost reached Brahma or escape from the Round of
birth and death except that he "met a lady, and . . .
sort of stopped meditating" (p. 188), that he had his
first mystical experience at the age of six when he
observed his sister drinking milk and suddenly realized
that she was God and the milk was God and everything was God, and that the apple Adam ate in the
Garden of Eden was logic.

Teddy's Vedantic beliefs are entirely in keeping
with the Zen that figures in all of the earlier stories,
and reinforce the rationale of the *koan* with which the
book begins, that truth eludes every attempt to catch
it by logic, which, as Teddy says, "is the first thing you
have to get rid of" (p. 190) if you want to get out of
the finite dimensions. Logic and "intellectual stuff"
have to be vomited up, Teddy argues, if we want to
see things correctly. And his theory of education
would be to show children how to meditate so that
they could find out who they are. "I'd just make them
vomit up every bit of the apple their parents and
everybody made them take a bite out of" (p. 196) is
what he would do if he had his way in the schools.

One of Teddy's least endearing abilities as far as
Nicholson is concerned is another part of his Vedantic
capabilities. Because of already having lived through a
thousand lives, Teddy is able to predict when he and
others will die. In fact, we learn from his notebook
that his own death will occur either on 14 February
1958, or on the very day he is talking to Nicholson. It

turns out to be the latter. Teddy concludes his talk with Nicholson, walks down to the empty swimming pool, looks over the edge, and is pushed to his death by his sister (a scene he has already outlined to Nicholson as a possibility of what might happen to him should he die that day).

"Teddy" is not by any means a nicely controlled story. Its characterization suffers from the same defects as those in "De Daumier-Smith's Blue Period." Teddy's mother and father are introduced, given some tantalizing development (Teddy's father, for instance, plays three leading roles simultaneously on daytime radio serials), and then dropped. And his sister is introduced as a mean child (because she has not had a chance to live very many lives, Teddy explains), but she comes across as simply cruel and it is difficult to think of her as at all believable. At best, the dialogue between Teddy and Nicholson reads like an awkward device to convey Salinger's religious philosophy; at its worst, it does little to encourage the reader to develop much sympathy for a character who is simply *too* wise. But the major thing wrong with the story is that it does not move. Its static quality is the consequence of contrast without conflict. As Kirschner comments, "Teddy hurries to his rendezvous with death, and the moral squalor of the rest of the family is all beside the point."[15]

Despite its weaknesses as a short story, "Teddy" is an appropriate conclusion to the collection. Not only does it provide a final commentary on the opening *koan*; it serves to explain and underline the point of Seymour's death in the first story, "A Perfect Day for Bananafish"—that for those like Seymour and Teddy who have experienced awakening by seeing through the absurdity of the logic that blinds "normal" people, physical death may be spiritual life. "Teddy" also works in another way to top off the structure of *Nine*

Stories by completing a sequence that begins with the despair over Seymour's ego-bemused society, moves toward an emphasis on provisional rescue through intuitive love for Sergeant X, and ends with Teddy's passage through the perimeters of personality.[16] It represents, as all of the stories do, "the sound of one hand clapping," and it does serve to show us the importance of moving beyond the easy laws of logic and being "raised to a higher level of awareness of the real *real* in worlds of tension, contradiction, paradox, humor, love, and squalor."[17]

Although *Nine Stories* received more perceptive and generally more positive reviews than did *The Catcher in the Rye*, most reviewers failed to notice much of a thematic pattern in the stories, and the importance of the opening *koan* in understanding the significance of Buddhist ideology in the stories was pretty much ignored. For example, Seymour Krim, writing in *Commonweal*, did not believe that Salinger is quite clear about the meaning of his material: "he is extremely deft, sometimes over-sophisticated in his surface technique, and for the most part it is a pure pleasure to follow his artistic strokes. But underneath, where it is a question of values and finally of the iron moral grasp of meaning, one suspects a dodging of issues."[18] Krim's objections were, of course, influenced by some of the admittedly weaker stories in the book as were Gene Baro's in the *New York Herald Tribune Book Review:* "Not all of these stories succeed, even despite Mr. Salinger's considerable skill in telling them. Though there is usually sensitive selection of detail, vivid dialogue, some spice of wit and irony, and almost always warmth of feeling, a few of these pieces seem uncommonly thin."[19]

But a few reviewers did hit on unifying factors in the stories. Eudora Welty, in the *New York Times*, pointed out the importance of seeing the stories as paradoxes: "J. D. Salinger's writing is original, first rate, serious and beautiful. Here are nine of his stories, and one further reason that they are so interesting, and so powerful seen all together, is that they are paradoxes. From the outside, they are often very funny; inside, they are all about heartbreak, and convey it; they can do this because they are pure."[20] Another reviewer who was willing to see the stories in their relationship to each other emphasized the unifying power of Salinger's use of irrelevant details as beatific signals: "Under their deceptively brilliant and lively surfaces, these pictures of over-wrought humanity are sharp and even important, particularly as they make telling use of frighteningly human irrelevant details."[21] And the excellence of the dialogue as it carries from story to story was something else for which the book was widely praised: "Mr. Salinger's greatest gift of all is an astonishing, almost perfectly disciplined capacity for dialogue. To reproduce functional, natural, and accurate conversation is one of the most difficult and demanding tasks a writer faces. Mr. Salinger sets the standard for excellence."[22]

No reviewer, however, saw the stories for what they really are metaphorically—as near-perfect examples of Zen art. Because of the Zen emphasis on "indirectness," on signs and symbols in expressing the nature of reality, art forms, particularly painting and poetry, are especially important in Zen. Salinger's awareness of Zen art is apparent in his stories. Two examples that spring immediately to mind are M. Yoshoto's painting of the white goose in the pale blue sky and Teddy's recitation of two Japanese poems (the only kind of poetry he can stand): "Nothing in the voice of the cicada intimates how soon it will die" and "Along this road goes no one, this autumn eve" (p. 185). And the impression left by each of his stories is similar to the feeling left by the calligraphic style of painting done with black ink on paper or silk that was practiced by Chinese artists as early as the eighth century, a form of painting in which the objective, as in a Salinger story, is unhesitating spontaneity, and where a single stroke is often enough to give away one's character, the picture itself designed to bring about *satori*.

Most Zen paintings are landscapes, but when Zen artists turned to representation of the Zen patriarchs and masters, they painted figures who very much resemble Salinger characters. The Patriarchs are represented for the most part as abandoned lunatics (think of Holden Caulfield as the lunatic in the tombs) who scowl, shout, loaf, and roar with laughter as they exemplify the glorious nonsense and emptiness of Zen life. In a comment that could just as well be about Salinger's Holden, Seymour, and Daumier-Smith, Watts explains that "In these lunatic figures the Zen artists portray something slightly more than a parody of their own *wu-shin* or "mindless" way of life, for 'as genius is to madness close allied' there is a suggestive parallel between the meaningless babble of the happy lunatic and the purposeless life of the Zen sage."[23]

The most obvious relationship between Zen art and Salinger's writing is, of course, between the "wordless" poetry of the *haiku* and the careful use of language in the stories. The *haiku*, which reached its fullest form in the seventeenth century, consists of just seventeen syllables, and tries, through a single image, to convey the same effect as Zen painting does through its use of empty space. "In poetry," emphasizes Watts, "the empty space is the surrounding silence which a two-line poem requires—a silence of the mind in which one does not 'think about' the poem but actually feels the sensation which it evokes—all the more strongly for having said so little."[24] The same effect is achieved by many of Salinger's stories. It is the silence we feel as much as anything at the end of "A Perfect Day for Bananafish," "The Laughing Man," and "Teddy," a silence that is the sound of one hand clapping.

Given the direct reference to Zen painting and poetry in *Nine Stories*, it is not surprising that the Zen practice that has evoked the most curiosity in the Western world, the tea ceremony, should figure in what most critics agree is the best-written story in the collection, "For Esmé—With Love and Squalor." In Buddhism, tea has nearly the same sacramental function as wine does in Christianity. Its slightly bitter yet clarifying taste is said to suggest the same taste as Buddhist awakening itself, and it has long been used by Zen monks as a stimulant for meditation. The ceremony (which dates for lay use since the fifteenth century and now involves at least three main "schools") consists of a ritualistic serving of the tea, drinking it, and then admiring the caddy, bowls, and utensils that are used. Included in the ceremony, which is frankly accepted as an escape from the concerns of business and worldly competition, is non-argumentative discussion of philosophical matters.[25] In Salinger's story there is no attempt at direct representation of the tea ceremony, but the Sergeant has entered the tearoom as an escape (both from the rain and the barracks), the experience does figure in his awakening, and he and Esmé do carry on a non-argumentative discussion that ultimately turns on the philosophical meaning of squalor—the very thing the tea ceremony enables one to escape.

If the tea ceremony is central to one of the most memorable stories of the book, perhaps it is not pushing the metaphor of Zen art and its influence on *Nine Stories* too far to point out that the overall arrangement is much like that found in a Japanese garden, where the attempt, as in the stories, is not to make a strictly realistic illusion of a miniature landscape, "but simply to suggest the general atmosphere of 'mountain and water' in a small space, so arranging the design of the garden that it seems to have been helped rather than governed by the hand of man."[26] The arrangement of Salinger's stories in the literal sense of the order in which they appear in the book seems to follow this principle. They give the impression of pattern and structure to the collection, yet the order is simply the order of magazine publication. They are arranged but they are not arranged. Another similarity between the stories and Zen gardening is in *bonseki*, the art of "discovering" rocks along the seashore and mountains that have been shaped by wind and water into living contours and then positioning them in the garden so that they look as if they have "grown" there. Salinger does much the same thing in his use of otherwise insignificant objects (a chicken sandwich, a red piece of waste paper, a watch) as beatific signs. And just as the Zen gardeners, Salinger is always sparing and reserved in his use of color.

Zen art requires incredible care and by its very nature cannot be prolific—something that must be taken into consideration in any discussion of Salinger's relatively "slight" output. Once a writer accepts the Zen principles of art, as Salinger's *Nine Stories* indicates he has, he becomes like the Zen gardener who can never cease to weed, prune, and train his plants, and who must do so with the realization that he is part of the garden himself, not some sort of controlling agent standing outside. This is what Salinger accomplishes in *Nine Stories*; he is so much inside the stories that they become an interior monologue in which we can perceive the writer's own movement toward *satori* as he faces the essential Zen fact of all that side of life completely beyond the control of logic. And how has he done this? Perhaps through gaining the same insight as the Zen master teaches in Eugene Herrigel's *Zen in the Art of Archery:* "What is true of archery and swordsmanship also applies to all the other arts. Thus, mastery in ink-painting is only attained when the hand, exercising perfect control over technique, executes what hovers before the mind's eye at the same moment when the mind begins to form it, without there being a hair's breadth between. Painting then becomes spontaneous calligraphy. Here again the painter's instructions might be: spend ten years observing bamboos, become a bamboo yourself, then forget everything and—paint."[27]

4

A Cloister of Reality:
The Glass Family

The important business for the writer of fiction is to place boundaries where, naturally, there are none. A short story or a novel is a limited, formal, artificial representation of the illimitable. The total of consciousness for the writer is like Leibnitz's sea wave whose murmur is made up of all the particular sounds produced by the droplets composing it. As Henry James cautions in the preface to *Roderick Hudson*, "Really, universally, relations stop nowhere, and the exquisite problem of the artist is eternally but *to draw, by a geometry of his own, the circle* within which they shall happily appear to do so."[1] What James means by *circle* is the necessary and arbitrary cutting-out accomplished by the artist in the great fluid mass of experience to create a cloister within which reality can be isolated, contemplated, and represented. For James this comes to be, in a whole series of novels, a matter of establishing a central point of view in the consciousness of a single character and then allowing that point of view to open onto a peripheral world. For Salinger in the work that follows *Nine Stories*, it is a matter of using a family of characters, the Glass family, and multiple—although closely related—points of view in order to delineate the sources of insight and stability that are his way of dealing with and adapting to the chaos of experience.

What seems to happen in Salinger's writing as we read through the later pieces in *Nine Stories*, especially "De Daumier-Smith's Blue Period" and "Teddy," is that, as much as he is concerned with the exigencies of Zen art, he develops a certain dissatisfaction with the short story form he employs in the earlier parts of the book. He demonstrates considerable impatience with the demands of secondary characterization, dialogues begin turning into monologues, and he violates one rule that Whit Burnett could never have accepted —he does more telling than showing. But this impatience is not with the limitations of the short story so much as it is a symptom of a search for centrality, a search for some means of inventing a universe whose frame will accord with his interpretive fancies in revealing the inner depths of the conscious, illuminated being. This centrality, this universe, finally becomes that of a Jewish-Irish couple and their seven brilliant and generally troubled children, and it is with these characters that Salinger has apparently been chiefly concerned for more than two decades.

In developing the so-called "Glass family saga," Salinger has become more than ever a literary ventriloquist, and he has been soundly (and perhaps deservedly) criticized for this. His tendency even when reproducing a letter written by the sainted Seymour at the age of seven in "Hapworth 16, 1924," is to talk *through* his characters rather than making them seem as if they are speaking *for* themselves. Even so, he does manage to make the members of the Glass family distinct enough so that each of them functions as a means of perceiving things according to the angle of incidence which the separate characters give their creator. At the back of the consciousness of Salinger's Glass family is thus the consciousness of Salinger himself, a little occult at times, and at other times too much in the foreground. To a certain extent, of course,

Salinger's writing takes on the qualities of an internal monologue early in his career; but it is only when he centers on the Glass family that the consciousness behind the monologue begins to emerge fully in dialogue with itself, even though many of the themes—the essential obscenity of modern life, the redeeming power of love, the Zen emphasis on transcending the ego—remain the same.

Salinger's interest in the Glass family is not, of course, limited to his last two books and his most recently published story. The most memorable character in *Nine Stories* is the Seymour of "A Perfect Day for Bananafish," his sister, Boo Boo, figures in the much weaker story, "Down at the Dinghy," and Walt Glass's peculiar use of language provides the title for "Uncle Wiggily in Connecticut." In fact, the details about the family are so scattered through Salinger's work that it is necessary for him to outline the family structure by means of a footnote in *Franny and Zooey* (p. 51).[2]

Les Glass and Bessie Gallagher, the parents, were popular Pantages Circuit vaudevillians in the 1920s—a career that has its obvious symbolic implications for the family, because there is a vaudevillian quality to the way Salinger depicts the Glasses. The very way he writes about them, constantly shifting the narrative voice and changing styles, and the way each of the family members is given his or her own genius suggests nothing so much as a stage show consisting of mixed specialty acts, including songs, dances, comic skits, and even acrobatic performances. By the 1940s, Les (who never figures directly in any of the stories) and Bessie (whose "fat Irish rose" of a personality is very prominent in *Franny and Zooey*) have ended their own performing careers, and Les is working as a talent scout for a motion picture studio in Los Angeles. By the 1950s, when *Franny and Zooey* takes place, they are living in an old but comfortable apartment

house in New York (the East Seventies) with their
two youngest children.

The oldest, Seymour, has long since committed
suicide, but his life does need some recounting. He
was born in February 1917, began attending Columbia
University when he was fifteen, graduated with a
Ph.D. in English, and taught for several years before
entering the Army Air Corps. On 4 June 1942, he married a girl named Muriel Fedder, whom he had met
while stationed at Fort Monmouth, New Jersey. Possibly because of his reaction to the psychoanalysis he
submitted to (under the pressure of Muriel and her
mother) after he got out of the Army, he purposely
drove the Fedders' car into a tree, and engaged in
other bizarre behavior. In the hope that he might re-
cover, he and Muriel took a vacation in Florida, where
they had spent their honeymoon. There, as we know
from "A Perfect Day for Bananafish," Seymour shot
himself on 18 March 1948.

Buddy, the brother with whom Seymour shared a
room in his parents' apartment until 1940 (the two
brothers then moved into an apartment of their own
near 79th and Madison), was born the same year as
was Salinger himself (it is significant that Salinger's
nickname as a child was "Sonny"), and grew up to be
the writer of the family, and Salinger's alter ego, as
well. Like Salinger, Buddy never finished college, and
he also entered the service when Salinger did, 1942. In
1955 he was a writer in residence teaching in upper
New York state at a women's junior college where he
lived alone in an unwinterized, unelectrified house.

The first girl born in the family is Boo Boo. As
Salinger describes her in "Down at the Dinghy," despite her joke of a name and her lack of prettiness, she
is "in terms of permanently memorable, immoderately
perceptive, small-area faces—a stunning and final girl"
(p. 77). Her adjustment to the world seems remark-

able for a Glass child. During the war, when she was a Wave stationed in Brooklyn, she met a steady, businesslike young man named Tannenbaum. By 1955, the Tannenbaums had three children, a summer place somewhere in New England, and a house in Tuckahoe.

The twins, Waker and Walt, were born after Boo Boo, and so far figure less in the family chronicle than even she does. Waker was a conscientious objector during the war, which he spent in a detention camp, and later became a Catholic priest. Walt, as we know from "Uncle Wiggily in Connecticut," spent World War II in the Pacific and was killed in the autumn of 1945 when a Japanese stove he was packing as a souvenir for his commanding officer exploded.

Zachary Martin Glass, known as Zooey, was born in 1929. The handsomest of the Glass children, he became a television actor after he graduated from college, much against the wishes of his mother who wanted him to follow up on his precocious abilities in Mathematics and Greek. Franny, the youngest, born in 1934, is as good-looking as Zooey, and like him is interested in acting, having played summer stock with great success between her junior and senior years in college.

Beginning in 1927 and continuing for seventeen years, at least one and sometimes more of the Glass children was regularly heard on a network radio program, "It's a Wise Child," a children's quiz show. All seven of them, with Seymour, of course, being the most prodigious, astounded their listeners with their ability to answer bookishly cute questions sent in from across the country. As Buddy explains in *Franny and Zooey*, the reaction of the listeners to the performances of the Glass children on the radio show resulted in a division into "two, curiously restive camps: those who held that the Glasses were a bunch of insufferable 'superior' little bastards that should have been drowned or gassed at birth, and those who held that they were bona-fide underage wits and savants, of an uncommon, if unenviable order" (p. 54). This might well be the same division that occurs among Salinger's readers as they get their first extended introduction to the Glass family in *Franny and Zooey*.

The book actually consists of two long stories put together into what almost, but not quite, becomes a novel. An abrupt shift in narrative technique from omniscient point of view in the first story (originally published in *The New Yorker*, 29 January 1955) to having Buddy serve as the narrator in the second (also published in *The New Yorker*, 4 May 1957) gives the book an awkward structure. But despite the narrative shift, the two stories are best considered as one unit, not only because the second story serves to resolve the first, but also because the two of them taken together mark an essential change in Salinger's fiction. Through his use of the Glass family as an organizing concept for his vision, and through his increased reliance on Buddy as the narrator in that portrayal, Salinger attempts to more firmly capture the paradoxical splendor and squalor of life, while concurrently presenting a vision of twentieth-century America that is ultimately positive. The source of that vision is something that comes as a relief after the occasional overemphasis on the efficacy of Oriental thought in *Nine Stories*, and Holden Caulfield's apparent attainment of Buddhahood at the end of *The Catcher in the Rye*. What we perceive through Salinger's ventriloquial act (his own vaudeville role, so to speak) is a deeper awareness engendered by the paradox itself—that there are no pat answers to the problems of existence —not even Zen—and that the paradox of splendor and squalor, or of the nice and the phony, can be resolved only through character and being. *Franny and Zooey* thus places emphasis on character rather than action, and clearly shows Salinger moving from the well-made structures of his early stories to the discursive narrative insights of Buddy Glass working from his position within the conceptual and focusing frame of the family.[3]

Franny and Zooey opens on the morning of the Yale game at an Ivy League school, with Lane Coutell, a pretentious senior English major of the sort who believes that someday he will own a hotline to *PMLA*, waiting on a railroad platform for Franny, his date for the weekend. Salinger quickly gives us two insights into Lane's character. The first is when one of his classmates in Modern European Literature wants to know what "this bastard Rilke is all about" (p. 6). Lane nonchalantly claims to understand the German-Bohemian poet (1875–1926), but it is soon apparent that someone with Lane's coldness of spirit could never comprehend Rilke's personal soliloquies, the *Duino Elegies*, which celebrate the poet's intense emotional reaction to his existence.[4] The second insight provided by Salinger reinforces the idea of coldness. When Franny's train arrives, Salinger delineates Lane's personality in a sentence that is a reminder of F. Scott Fitzgerald at his best: "Then, like so many people, who, perhaps ought to be issued only a very probational pass to meet trains, he tried to empty his face of all expressions that might quite simply, perhaps even beautifully, reveal how he felt about the arriving person" (p. 7).

Franny, by contrast, greets Lane warmly, but she immediately feels guilty about expressing affection for him, and Salinger carefully establishes a mood in which both partners sense that everything is unaccountably going wrong with their weekend from the start. They go for lunch to a restaurant called Sickler's, a place where one was careful to order snails, not

steak. Lane holds forth pompously, and Franny soon
realizes that he epitomizes the self-centered, pseudo-
intellectual qualities that have caused her to become
hypersensitive and acutely critical of people like him.
"I'm just so sick of pedants and conceited little tearer-
downers I could scream," she says (p. 17). They get
into an argument over poets and poetry, and in the
first of several discussions concerning bad writing versus good writing that is almost a major theme in the
last two books, Franny says, "I don't *know* what a real
poet is. . . . I know this much, is all. If you're a poet,
you do something beautiful. I mean you're supposed
to *leave* something beautiful after you get off the page
and everything" (p. 19). The poets she knows on the
faculty of her college do not do this; they simply leave
what she calls "syntaxy *droppings.*"

This discussion literally makes her sick. She ex-
cuses herself from the table and goes to the ladies'
room, where she breaks down and cries. She takes a
little green book she has been carrying with her out of
her purse and presses it to her chest, regaining her
composure almost at once. She returns to the table and
tries to explain what is bothering her. The main problem is ego and self-centeredness. She tells Lane that
she has even dropped out of the play she was in because she could not stand all the ego. "All I know is
I'm losing my mind," she tells Lane. "I'm just sick of
ego, ego, ego" (p. 29). And then she reluctantly begins
to tell him about the little green book, *The Way of a
Pilgrim*, written by a Russian peasant in the nineteenth century who wanders across his country until
he meets a *starets*, a seer who teaches him a method of
praying without ceasing. The method involves repeating the "Jesus Prayer"—"Lord Jesus Christ, have
mercy on me"—until the prayer becomes self-active,
and *something* happens: "You do it to purify your
whole outlook and get an absolutely new conception

of what everything's about" (p. 37). The same process is used in Hinduism, Buddhism, and other religions to gain a sense of religious peace and transcend the self, but it means nothing to Lane. As Franny talks about *The Way of a Pilgrim,* he is intent on dissecting the froglegs that are on his plate, and tries to shut her up by asking her if she really believes in that stuff. She replies that it is a way of seeing God: "Something happens in some absolutely nonphysical part of the heart—where the Hindus say that Atman resides, if you ever took any religion—and you see God, that's all" (p. 39). Lane may have taken some religion, but he seems incapable of responding to religious ideas, looks at his watch, and ironically says, "God. We don't have time" (p. 40). He means that they might not be able to get to the game on time, but he also indicates that he has no time for Franny's mysticism concerning apprehending the divine. He tries to tell her that religious experiences of the type she describes all have a simple psychological explanation.

Franny cannot take anymore. She tries to return to the ladies' room but faints before she can get there. She wakes up on a couch in the restaurant manager's office with Lane looking down at her and saying that he is going to take her to the room that he has reserved for her. And then, in his selfishness and blindness (also revealing that they have been lovers), he assures her that he will later try to sneak up the back staircase. He leaves to get a cab, and the first part of the book ends as Franny begins mumbling the Jesus Prayer.

The Way of a Pilgrim and the Jesus Prayer are by no means being put forth as answers to anything by Salinger. Franny has reached the point of a nervous breakdown as Lane leaves her on the couch, and the Jesus Prayer is no solution to her problem. A major idea in Zen (and also in Plato's parable of the cave, and even in Emerson's Perennial Philosophy) is that people who are too critical of others, who are too concerned with the analysis of particulars, fail to reach an understanding of the oneness of all things, and eventually disintegrate themselves.[5] This is what has happened to Franny, and the Jesus Prayer serves only to lead her deeper into her paranoid and hypercritical withdrawal from reality.

The condition Salinger leaves Franny in as she is lying on the couch (a condition that continues on into the second part of the book) indicates that Salinger has become more committed to what might be called the "wait" than to the "quest." Franny is a victim of her fate, not a ruler over it, and her subsequent experience becomes a "downward path to wisdom."[6] From this point on in the story, Salinger pays minimal attention to plot. As in *The Fall* by Camus and *Waiting for Godot* by Beckett, conversation, self-analysis, and the search for meaning within the experience become more important than what happens, and extreme care is exerted to avoid pretending that value exists where it does not.

Franny's search for meaning involves, of course, the dissolution of opposites—good and evil, squalor and splendor, the nice and the phony—that figures so often in Salinger's fiction and is an inevitable result of Salinger's interest in Zen. The Zen neophyte (which so many of his characters, including Franny, resemble) begins by thinking about rational solutions to apparent opposites, including the distinction between self and others, and ultimately reaches an impasse that is created by the struggling ego. When the neophyte "lets go," gives up the struggle, and no longer distinguishes between acting and being acted upon, he is on the way to enlightenment. Once he has reached this state, he is free to be fully acted upon in every action he performs, and this means complete absorption in the process of loss of ego. As we have seen, many of Salinger's stories seem to be structured around producing this experience in some of his characters. Franny is thus a typical Salinger character on the road to enlightenment, wrestling with the problem of burdensome ego, isolated by continual criticism of others and of herself, something that is, in fact, the central dichotomy of the younger Glasses.[7]

But her enlightenment is no simple process and it cannot be seen merely as another dialogue between Zen master and pupil with an easily discernible (if not solvable) *koan* at the center. Nor is it described by means of a tightly structured narrative as her experience in the "Franny" part of the book is. The "Zooey" section is narrated by Buddy, who opens by saying that he is not giving us a short story at all but "a sort of prose home movie" (p. 47), with what plot there is hinging on "mysticism, or religious mystification" (p. 48). The story does have some of the qualities of a home movie because it conveys the impression of an unedited glimpse into the private, and occasionally awkward, moments of life in the Glass household. The idea of the prose home movie is a dangerous metaphor, however, because home movies when viewed at length are finally of interest only to those who see themselves or someone they know intimately on the screen. And the effect often is one of self-indulgence, just the criticism repeatedly directed at Salinger's work from the "Zooey" section on. One does get the feeling in reading the later books that their final charm may be reserved, just as home movies are, for a chosen few or an inner group of initiates. As Buddy says of the leading characters in the story, Franny, Zooey, their mother Bessie, and himself, "We speak a kind of esoteric, family language, a sort of semantic geometry in which the shortest distance between any two points is a fullish circle" (p. 49).

As round-about as the dialogue in the story is, and as esoteric (and precious) as it sometimes seems, it does add up to a ventriloquist's act through which Salinger moves Franny toward a moment of self-transcendence that is as satisfying as anything in his fiction. But the process begins in indirectness and unwinds like an 8 mm film that has been spliced together at the kitchen table. After making his disclaimer at the start, Buddy introduces Zooey, who is reading a four-year-old letter from Buddy, in the bathtub, and Buddy then says that he will refer to himself in the third-person throughout the rest of the story. This does not give us quite the narrative stance that we have in "Franny," however. The presence of Buddy is felt during the rest of the story, and there is a sympathetic, insider's tone that gives the narrative more warmth and authenticity than we find in "Franny."

Buddy reproduces the letter in its entirety, and through it we can see the role he and Seymour played in educating Franny and Zooey—an education Zooey is not altogether satisfied with. After expressing his reservations about Zooey's choice of acting as a career, Buddy tries to explain why he and Seymour took over the instruction of the youngest members of the family so high-handedly. Because of the brilliance of Franny and Zooey on the quiz show, both Seymour and Buddy began to worry that the two child prodigies would turn into "academic weisenheimers." Seymour had become convinced, through his reading in Zen, that education should not begin with a quest for knowledge but with a quest for "no-knowledge," the realization that the state of pure consciousness known as *satori* involves being with God before he said, "Let there be light." So the prescribed reading included

Max Mueller's *Sacred Books of the East,* and Franny and Zooey grew up knowing more about Jesus and Gautama and Lao-tse and Shankaracharya and Hui-neng and Sri Ramakrishna than they did about Homer or Shakespeare or George Washington. All of this had so much impact on Zooey at one time that he tried to get over an unhappy love affair by translating the Mundaka Upanishad into classical Greek.

Buddy apologizes for not following up on this early instruction after the death of Seymour, and explains that what prompted the letter was hearing a little girl in a supermarket say she has two boyfriends, "Bobby and Dorothy." This reminded him of Seymour's observation that all legitimate religious study leads to unlearning the illusory differences between boys and girls, day and night, and heat and cold. But this is not easy to unlearn, and the instruction has hardly been beneficial to Franny and Zooey—Franny has suffered an incipient nervous breakdown and Zooey has an ulcer.

Zooey puts the letter away and picks up a script for a television play he has been reading, when Bessie, dressed in a kimono and a hairnet, comes into the bathroom and opens the medicine cabinet. Here we are given a long list of what is in the cabinet—from Ex-Lax to three tickets to a 1946 musical comedy, "Call Me Mister." The list is distracting and does not seem necessary, but it functions (as do the later catalogs of the contents of the Glass family living room and the bulletin-board collection of famous quotations in Seymour and Buddy's room) not only to continue the prose home movie idea, but also to emphasize that there are objects, furnishings, and ideas that have an existence—are *there*—independent of the internalized concerns of the ego. This cataloging tendency continues through the next book and emphasizes the point that while it is necessary to see through external reality, it is still there, still real, and must be dealt with before any transcendence can take place.

Zooey carries on a long and irritable conversation with his mother from behind the bath curtain (another example of Salinger characters not addressing each other directly—it is as if there is a bath curtain separating all of them). Bessie is a great worrier, but her worry at the moment concerns Franny. Bessie wants Zooey to find out what is bothering his sister. Since she got home on Saturday night (it is now Monday morning), she has kept to the couch, has been unable to eat, and remains silent and withdrawn. Bessie does suspect, however, that the little green book might have something to do with Franny's condition, and Zooey indicates that she could not have made a better guess. He tells her that the book and a sequel to it, "The Pilgrim Continues His Way," came out of Seymour and Buddy's bedroom, and it is because of Seymour and Buddy's educational system that both he and Franny are especially susceptible to such ideas. "We're *freaks*, the two of us, Franny and I," he announces. "I'm a twenty-five-year-old freak and she's a twenty-year-old freak, and both those bastards are responsible. . . . The symptoms are a little more delayed in Franny's case than mine, but she's a freak, too, and don't you forget it. I swear to you, I could murder them both without even batting an eyelash. The great teachers. The great emancipators. My God. I can't even sit down to lunch with a man any more and hold up my end of a decent conversation" (pp. 103–104). And he adds that he cannot even sit down to a meal without first saying "The Four Great Vows" of Buddhism under his breath: "However innumerable beings are, I vow to save them; however inex*haust*ible the passions are, I vow to extinguish them; however immeasurable the Dharmas are, I vow to master them; however incomparable the Buddha-truth is, I vow to *attain* it" (pp. 104–105). Instead of being enlighten-ing, the four vows have become obsessive.

With this attitude, Zooey ends his talk with Bes-sie, gets dressed, and goes into the living room to wake Franny up. Near the start of the dialogue, Zooey no-tices some sheet music on a stand. A sepia reproduc-tion of Mr. and Mrs. Glass in top hat and tails is featured on the cover, and the title, "You Needn't Be So Mean, Baby," functions for Zooey as a beatific sig-nal. He tells Franny that one problem with both of them is that they have "Wise Child" complexes, that they both cannot stop picking at others because of their own sense of superiority. He accuses her of using the Jesus Prayer for egotistical purposes, for laying up spiritual treasures for herself, without even praying to the "real" Jesus. He reminds her of the time when she was ten and came rushing into his room with a Bible in her hand saying she could no longer believe in Jesus because of the way he threw the tables around in the synagogue and because he said that human beings are more valuable to God than the fowls of the air. At that point, Zooey says, she quit the Bible and went straight to Buddha because of her inability to understand any son of God who might actually have said and done the things attributed to him. And now in using the name *Jesus* as a *mantra* in the Jesus Prayer with the idea, recognized in most meditative religions, that repetition of a word or phrase until it is automatic will lead to escape from external reality, she is continuing that tendency. But the Jesus Prayer that Jesus himself might have advocated would have a different aim— "To endow the person who says it with Christ-Consciousness. *Not* to set up some little cozy, holier-than-thou trysting place with some sticky, adorable divine *pers*onage who'll take you in his arms and re-lieve you of all your duties and make all your nasty *Weltschmerzen* . . . go away and never come back" (p.

172). Wholesale adoption of the Jesus Prayer as a mantra is dangerous, Zooey explains, because it is entirely possible for someone to be blissfully reciting it while robbing the poorbox. Real Christ-Consciousness involves the realization that "You Needn't Be So Mean, Baby."

What Zooey is getting at here is the old problem of dichotomies in Salinger's thought. Religious mysticism can be nice, but it can also be phony. At the time the stories were written, Zen had become not only fashionable but downright faddish as had other mystical ways of seeking transcendence, and the dialogue between Franny and Zooey seems clearly to be a reaction to this phenomenon. Seymour may have reached the state of enlightenment through his studies in Oriental wisdom, and Buddy may nearly have gotten there, but for Franny it has led to a breakdown and for Zooey an anxiety-caused illness. What Salinger is doing is something that seems inevitable in American thought. He is cautioning that we must take pragmatism into account in judging any religious approach or philosophical notion. We should ask the question, does it work? Simple mysticism simply accepted does not. Nor does an educational approach that *forces* the learning of the East on unsuspecting subjects as the young Franny and Zooey were.

Retreat from external reality, whether it be undertaken simple-mindedly through the Jesus Prayer or the necessity of it forced upon us by would-be gurus, can be just as phony as blindly pursuing material wealth and pleasure. And besides, Zooey realizes that external reality is not always so bad, and it is a mistake to lose touch with it. In the midst of his discussion with Franny, Zooey looks out the window and sees a little girl playing a trick on her dachshund. She is hiding behind a tree waiting for the dog to pick up her scent and find her. When the dog does, the two experience an immense and playful reunion. Zooey cannot help saying, "God damn it, there are nice things in the world—and I mean *nice* things. We're all such morons to get so sidetracked. Always, always, always referring every goddam thing that happens right back to our lousy little egos" (p. 152).

Franny starts to cry, and Zooey realizes he is not getting anywhere with her, perhaps because he is being too critical. He goes into Seymour and Buddy's room, where Seymour's separate-listing telephone has been kept all these years. He sits in front of the telephone with a white handkerchief on his head and thinks for awhile. Then he picks up the phone, dials the apartment telephone, disguises his voice as Buddy's, and asks to speak to Franny. He makes use of his acting ability not to draw attention to himself, nor to flatter his own ego as most actors do, but instead he acts out of kindness, out of concern for Franny. He thinks it will help her if she can hear Buddy's voice, but he makes a slip and she recognizes him. He tells her that she can go on with the Jesus Prayer, that he has no right to criticize her, but that she should realize that the only thing that counts in religious life of any sort is *detachment* and selflessness. But she should realize that "desirelessness" is not the same thing and is not necessarily good. It is her desiring to be an actress that has made her a good one. "You're stuck with it now," he reminds her. "You can't just *walk out* on the results of your own hankerings. Cause and effect, buddy, cause and effect" (p. 198). So what can she do? For her, he says, the only religious thing she can do is to *act*: "Act for God, if you want to—be God's actress, if you want to" (p. 198). But what she cannot do is act for herself, for her own ego, or even rave about the stupidity of the audiences. She has to act selflessly in the theatre, the world, as it is. This is part of Christ-Consciousness, something the Jesus Prayer can never give her.

He tries to explain to her what this means in another way by telling her how he resisted shining his shoes before one performance of "It's a Wise Child" because he thought the studio audience, the announcer, and the sponsors were all morons. Not only that, his shoes could not even be seen by the audience from where he sat. Seymour heard all this and told him to shine them anyway, to shine them for the "Fat Lady." Seymour did not tell him who she was, and Zooey had a picture in his mind of a cancerous woman sitting on her porch all day swatting flies and listening to the radio, but it somehow all made sense to him, and he shined his shoes. Franny confesses that Seymour had said the same thing to her. Zooey says to her that he is going to tell her a terrible secret. *"There isn't anyone out there who isn't Seymour's Fat Lady,"* he says. "That includes your Professor Tupper, buddy. And all his goddam cousins by the dozens. There isn't anyone *any*where that isn't Seymour's Fat Lady. Don't you know that? Don't you know that goddam secret yet? And don't you know—*listen* to me, now—*don't you know who that Fat Lady really is?* . . . Ah, buddy. Ah, buddy. It's Christ Himself. Christ Himself, buddy" (pp. 201–202).

This emphasis on the need to give love to others, on the need to practice a selfless and lonely benevolence, gives Franny a sudden moment of joy, a *satori* based not on retreat from external reality but of acceptance of her place within it. Like the Sergeant at the end of "For Esmé—with Love and Squalor," she falls into a deep dreamless sleep, the squalor in her life resolved through love.

But we must be careful in reading this story not to assume that Salinger is naively advocating the acceptance of Christianity through Zooey's long discussion of the nature of Christ and the incarnation of Jesus in the Fat Lady. If we look at the story this way, as an argument for Christianity, the resolution of Franny's breakdown at the end appears to be too sudden and without clear explanation. It is difficult to see how Zooey's theological and ethical arguments, taken simply by themselves, could bring about a conversion in anyone as intelligent as Franny is. We must remember, however, that despite his attack on the Jesus Prayer, Salinger is still writing with the Zen ideas found in *Nine Stories* in mind, although considerably more cautiously expressed, in *Franny and Zooey*. What happens at the end of the book is quite in keeping with Zen teachings. Zen enlightenment is often the result of a ridiculous gesture of the master or an absurd answer to a serious question. So one way of understanding the ending is to realize that Franny gets over her break-down by the very absurdity of Zooey's equation of Christ and the Fat Lady.[8] Salinger thus does not prescribe an all-encompassing love for the predicament of modern man, but suggests that the solution lies in the Christ-Consciousness that is the result of enlightenment through absurdity.

This positive view of the possibilities for enlightenment amid the splendor and squalor of modern life does not depend, however, on an acceptance of either the ideas of Zen or the beliefs of Christianity. It is a statement in favor of seeking the ultimate solution through character. *Franny and Zooey* lacks overt rendering of action. In fact, the single most dramatic action is Franny's falling asleep at the end. But through dialogue, Salinger has Buddy show us how Franny moves away from the pat answer of the Jesus Prayer to the moment of release when she overcomes the problem of ego. Her enlightenment represents a growth in character that is permitted and encouraged by the family circle within which it takes place and which affords a range of possibilities. "Everybody in this family gets his goddam religion in a different package," Zooey says (p. 154). But the problem for all of them is to deal with hyper-criticism, with the ego. And this is the message they all apparently sooner or later discover out of the legacy of Seymour's wisdom and the fact of his suicide.

The message does not arrive very speedily or with much economy of statement. And the same commentary might be made on the entire "Zooey" part of the book that is made about the letter from Buddy that is read in the bathtub: "virtually endless in length, overwritten, teaching, repetitious, opinionated, remonstrative, condescending, embarassing—and filled to a surfeit with affection" (p. 56). It is difficult to defend the book structurally other than to use Buddy's metaphor of the prose home movie (a metaphor that implies a lack of structure), and the book did come as something of an embarassment to readers who had defended and admired the earlier books. But *Franny and Zooey* has an unusual quality in contemporary fiction—it deals with characters the author actually *likes.* At times there may indeed be a surfeit of affection, but the affection nonetheless is transferable to the reader. Earnestness is, of course, no justification for a lack of style and structure, but the narrative warmth that comes through this book justifies Salinger's use of the Glass family as a means of delineating the sources and range of his insight and stability.

Salinger's love for the Glasses left some reviewers uneasy, however. John Updike, for instance, writing in the *New York Times Book Review,* objected to the uncomplementary jangle of the book's two parts, and then complained that "Salinger loves the Glasses . . . too exclusively. . . . He loves them to the detriment of artistic moderation."⁹ And in stronger language, Alfred Kazin went at much the same thing in the *Atlantic*. The Glass children are not only "cute," he wrote, but they "do not trust anything or anyone but themselves and their great idea. And what troubles me about this is not what it reflects of their theology but what it does to Salinger's art."¹⁰

But just as many, if not more, critics were taken by the book's warmth, although the seeming lack of control remained disturbing. *Time* responded to Kazin's charge by stating, "Critics . . . have suggested that the Glass children are too cute and too possessed by self-love. The charge is unjust. They are too clearly shadowed by death, even in their wooliest, most kittenish moments, to be cute, and they are too seriously worried about the very danger of self-love to be true egotists."¹¹ The very tenderness of the book appealed to the reviewer in *The Christian Century*: "The cumulative effect is bright and tender rather than powerful, and poignant rather than deep: these are the strengths and limitations of Salinger as a writer. These granted, he has an almost Pauline understanding of the necessity, nature, and redemptive quality of love. In Salinger, probably more than in any other serious contemporary writer of fiction, the modern college generation seems to find a mirror of its problems."¹² It was the treatment of love that also impressed A. E. Mayhew in *Commonweal*: "These two stories are about love. . . . For all their faults, they have a pleasing toughness and positiveness in their intent, something more than the verbal sleight-of-hand for which Salinger is justly famous."¹³ Granville Hicks, in *The Saturday Review*, replied to the many attacks on the book by writing that "Some critics have charged him with priggishness, and have said that he always has to put his heroes and heroines in the right. This is manifestly untrue. He dares to create characters who have virtue as their goal, but both Franny and Zooey are agonizingly conscious of their shortcomings, and both have a horror of self-righteousness. . . . In *Franny and Zooey* he is at the top of his form."[14]

Hicks was one of the few critics who could come out so glowingly for *Franny and Zooey*. The hesitations over Salinger's sudden prolixity were behind most of the reactions to the book, and many commentators flatly did not like what they sensed to be a shift in Salinger's narrative technique. Most of these hesitations were validated, so it seemed, when *Raise High the Roof Beam, Carpenters; and Seymour: An Introduction* was published in 1963. This is partly because the book is somewhat similar in structure to *Franny and Zooey*. The first section consists of a story (originally published in *The New Yorker*, 19 November 1955) complete with plot and even something of a resolution, and the second section (*The New Yorker*, 6 June 1959) is a dialogue of sorts between Buddy and Seymour (or rather, Seymour's ghost) that serves peripherally as a commentary on the first story, provides us, as the title indicates, with more information on Seymour, and finally comes down to a discussion of the nature of art, the crucial differences between poetry and prose, and the predicament of the artist. But even though both sections are this time narrated by Buddy, the two parts of the book do not fit together tightly, and "Seymour: An Introduction" comes about as close to being an essay as a piece of fiction can. However, the overall effect is one of intended delight. As in *Franny and Zooey*, Salinger is clearly writing about characters for whom he feels great affection because of the way they provide him with a means of centralizing his vision. And the antiform style that emerges in "Zooey" and to a much greater extent in "Seymour" need not be seen as a negative development or as "the self-indulgence of a writer flirting with depths of wisdom."[15] Ihab Hassan suggests a useful approach in pointing out that Salinger's later style may be understood as a metaphor of his sacramental and celebrational view of life: a work of art is an act of faith, and the act itself is a celebration.[16]

Indeed, "Raise High the Roof Beam, Carpenters" centers on sacrament and celebration, although ironically at first. It deals with Seymour's wedding to Muriel, but Seymour does not appear, and Buddy, the only member of the Glass family who is able to be present for the ceremony, is forced into a car with four other wedding guests to be driven to the apartment of the bride's parents for what has turned out to be a non-wedding reception. The situation Salinger utilizes to build his story around is a classic one in vaudeville and burlesque humor (First woman: "I heard you had a lovely wedding." Second woman: "Yes, it was wonderful. I was so happy. But it would have been even lovelier had my husband showed up"). Salinger makes the most of the humorous possibilities in Buddy's predicament with the other guests, one of whom is the Matron of Honor, not knowing at first who he is. The Matron of Honor is, of course, incensed at Seymour and talks on and on about how Muriel's mother ought now to be more than ever convinced that Seymour is a latent homosexual and a schizoid personality. What kind of a man, she asks, would keep his bride up until five in the morning the day of the wedding, as Seymour reportedly did, to tell her he is too *happy* to get married? Buddy's uncomfortable response to this line of conversation makes the Matron of Honor suspicious, and she guesses that he is Seymour's brother.

The car is stopped by a policeman to let a detail of Sea Scouts march by, and as the delay continues and the heat inside the car becomes unbearable, the passengers decide to walk to a nearby Schrafft's for a soda. Buddy learns that one of the other guests, a little old man who sits staring straight ahead with an unlit cigar in his mouth and a top hat on his head, is a deaf mute. They have to write him a note to ask if he wants to go along. He answers with one word: "Delighted." The Schrafft's is closed for alterations, so Buddy invites the others to his air-conditioned apartment, just a few blocks away, to escape the heat. When they get there, Buddy can stand the Matron of Honor's criticisms no longer, and he tells her that no one has seen Seymour for what he is—a poet. The Matron of Honor's only response is to ask if she can use the telephone so she can call the Fedders and explain the delay. In showing her into the bedroom where the telephone is, Buddy sees Seymour's diary and picks it up. He goes into the bathroom with it and there sees wedding congratulations written by Boo Boo (she had been staying in the apartment while Buddy and Seymour, both in the service, were at their army posts) in soap on the mirror. The message, which gives the story its title, is a verse from Sappho: "Raise high the roof beams, carpenters. Like Ares comes the bridegroom, taller far than a tall man" (p. 76). What follows next is a reproduction of parts of the diary, which was written when Seymour was stationed at Fort Monmouth in late 1941 and early 1942. Buddy is somewhat dismayed to learn that Seymour loves Muriel for her "undiscriminating heart." It is her lack of ego, her willingness to be uncritical that Seymour likes about her—a lesson that Buddy as narrator had not yet learned. Seymour writes about the growing suspicion Mrs. Fedder has that he is a schizoid personality. She is particularly disturbed over his reply to her question about what he intended to do when the war was over. His answer: He would like to be a dead cat. Mrs. Fedder thought he was making some kind of sophisticated joke, and her laughter distracted Seymour so much that he forgot to explain what he meant. He later told Muriel the point of the remark was that, as a Zen master once said, a dead cat is the most valuable thing in the world because no one could put a price on it.

Mrs. Fedder's suspicions continue to grow despite Muriel's explanation to her of what Seymour had actually meant by the dead-cat business, and she arranges to have her analyst present for dinner one night when Seymour is there. The analyst grills Seymour, coming down finally to a question about why Seymour was forced off "It's a Wise Child." The analyst had the impression that Seymour had said over the air that the Gettysburg Address was harmful to children. What he had said is that it is a bad speech for children to have to memorize because there had been 51,112 casualties at Gettysburg, and that if someone had to speak, the only appropriate response would have been to shake his fist at the audience and walk off the platform. Out of love for Muriel and to set Mrs. Fedder at ease, Seymour does agree to submit to psychoanalysis, but he has already diagnosed his condition: "Oh, God, if I'm anything by a clinical name, I'm a kind of paranoiac in reverse. I suspect people of plotting to make me happy" (p. 88).

Buddy slams the diary shut at the word *happy*. He feels betrayed, and there is more than a hint of jealousy in his reaction to the news that Seymour actually loves Muriel, and that he looks upon his marriage as almost a rebirth through the assumption of responsibility. Boo Boo in her wedding note intuitively indicates that she recognizes Seymour's motive as a desire to share the life of common mortals—but she also indicates something more ominous, that ordinary life and institutions will have to be generously expanded (the roofbeams raised) to accomodate the heroic proportions of Seymour. But Buddy as a writer of fiction instinctively reacts against this idea because he cannot believe in a happy ending so easily achieved.

When we first encounter Seymour in "A Perfect Day for Bananafish," we wonder how he could ever have married Muriel. In "Raise High the Roof Beam, Carpenters," we can understand how it happened, but we are also led to think of a few literary parallels involving the love-matches of genius-heroes—King Arthur and Guinevere, Dante and Beatrice, Faust and Gretchen, and, probably the most direct parallel, Gatsby and Daisy. In all of these examples, the hero is attracted to a woman who represents innocence and purity that is perceived by the lover, at any rate, as a lack of ego and a willingness to love him wholly and freely despite the burden of genius. And in every case, the consequences are disastrous. Mundane life is mundane life and cannot be expanded to accomodate the hero. External reality, as Zooey tells Franny, is inescapably *there*, and the tragedy of genius is to assume that it can be altered.

Many readers of Salinger have assumed that Seymour is to be understood as an unquestioned saint within the Glass family, a seer whose wisdom is final. To be certain, his personality, his diaries, his poems, his sayings, are with every member of the Glass family all the time, but not always as a positive force. Zooey and Buddy are in the process of rebelling *against* Seymour. In one sense, Seymour's suicide is justifiable. It is entirely acceptable within the Zen context *Nine Stories* provides. But outside of that context and from the point-of-view of Zooey, an actor, and Buddy, a writer, it becomes tragic. Seymour makes the same mistake Gatsby does—he idealizes a woman and isolates her conceptually from the reality that surrounds her. Gatsby overlooks the fact of Daisy's marriage and wants to ignore the existence of her daughter. Seymour discounts the presence of Muriel's family, especially her mother, and fails to see what they will do to him—they will not raise the roof beam; they intend to lower it.

The whole concept of Seymour as a Gatsby-figure is reinforced by the atmosphere of the gathering in Buddy's apartment. It is similar to the scene in *The Great Gatsby* where Gatsby, Daisy, Tom, Jordon, and Nick motor in from Long Island on a hot summer day and spend the afternoon drinking in the parlor of a suite in the Plaza Hotel room. The discussion revolves around the idea of happiness, and Gatsby's unwillingness to face reality is contrasted by Tom's matter-of-fact attitude that what is, is, and we can no more will to be happy than we can bring the past back.

Buddy emerges from the bathroom, serves his guests some Tom Collinses, and belts down several shots of whiskey. The Matron of Honor returns from the telephone and says all is well, Seymour and Muriel have eloped. All of the guests leave except the little old man who raises his glass to Buddy in salute. He suddenly becomes a symbol of death, reminiscent of the old man at the crossroads in Chaucer's "The Pardoner's Tale," grinning indifferently as Buddy tries to explain and justify Seymour's peculiar behavior. Buddy passes out, a premonition of Seymour's tragedy hanging over him. When he awakens, the old man is gone, the only trace of his presence an empty *glass* and a cigar end in a pewter ashtray. "I still think his cigar end should have been forwarded on to Seymour, the usual run of wedding gifts being what it is," Buddy concludes. "Just the cigar, in a small, nice box. Possibly with a blank sheet of paper enclosed, by way of explanation" (p. 107).

The empty glass and the cigar end function the same way as do the beatific signs in the earlier stories, but here the import is more subtle. Buddy achieves understanding at the end of "Raise High the Roof Beam, Carpenters," but it is not the kind that allows him to drift off into a dreamless and restorative sleep as do Sergeant X and Franny. The word *glass* is a crucial one for Buddy to use at the end, because he is not seeing through the glass the way Daumier-Smith looks through the window in a blaze of illumination. Buddy is seeing through the glass darkly as he realizes the difficulties in understanding the meaning of Seymour's presence in his own life and in that of his brothers and sisters. But as the glass darkens, the pattern of Salinger's saga of the Glass family becomes more clear. Seymour is a catalyst who changes others but does not himself undergo change. He teaches Buddy, Zooey, and Franny to be realists, naturalists, and humanists, even though he is a Zen-master, mystic, seer, and Christ-figure himself, with standards so high, so out-of-this-world that he cannot survive.[17] He is also a fool, a Gatsby-type who, through his fatal example, teaches the other characters that they must move toward compromise if they are to have a philosophy they can live by.

It is the idea of compromise that Buddy is mulling over at the age of forty when "Seymour: An Introduction" begins. He is speculating about his own career as a writer, a career that at first does seem like a considerable compromise when contrasted to that of Seymour. Buddy is a writer of fiction who must worry about communicating with the "general reader." Seymour, on the other hand, was a poet, a *mukta*, an enlightened man, a "true artist-seer, the heavenly fool who can and does produce beauty, [and] is mainly dazzled to death by his own scruples" (p. 123). What Buddy does in the long, rambling monologue that follows is to define his and Seymour's contrasting temperaments, and also to attempt the resolution of the contradictory impulses that beset the artist. Because of his very genius, his talent and sensitivity, the artist stands apart from the common lot of men. This is certainly Seymour's case, and he made no attempt to publish his poetry (Buddy has one of Seymour's notebooks with 184 poems in it—all the poems greatly influenced by Chinese and Japanese tradition, of course). But if the artist submits his work to the public, it is another matter. And this is Buddy's case. Once he publishes and performs before his audience, he involves himself in their lives and is forced to acknowledge a responsibility to others.

Buddy's agonizing over problems in communication, his relationship to his reader, and the writer's inherent moral dilemma also is Salinger's. This is underscored by the two quotations that precede the story, one by Kafka, one by Kierkegaard. The quotation from Kafka is:

The actors by their presence always convince me, to my horror, that most of what I've written about them until now is false. It is false because I write about them with steadfast love (even now, while I write it down, this, too, becomes false) but varying ability, and this varying ability does not hit off the real actors loudly and correctly but loses itself dully in this love that never will be satisfied with the ability and therefore thinks it is protecting this ability from exercising itself. (p. 111)

This is Kafka at his paradoxical and contradictory best (or worst), but what he is saying is something that comes out more and more as Salinger writes about the Glass family. That is, the characters of a writer, once created, take on a reality of their own that the writer must respect even to the point of protecting it from his own craft, which through its very artifice can falsify. Salinger's love for his characters overwhelms his simple storytelling techniques and encourages the personae of the Glass family to emerge all the more convincingly. The writer's craft is, as it were, broken by his own creation; but when this happens, his vision takes on new largeness and strangeness. It is not easy to predict what "Seymour: An Introduction" is to lead toward, but Helen Weinberg comments, "The story is governed by a sense of breakthrough and experiment."[18]

The quotation from Kierkegaard further enunciates the nature of Salinger's breakthrough:

It is (to describe it figuratively) as if an author were to make a slip of the pen, and as if this clerical error became conscious of being such. Perhaps this was no error, but in a far higher sense was an essential part of the whole exposition. It is, then, as if this clerical error were to revolt against the author, out of hatred for him, were to forbid him to correct it, and were to say, "No, I will not be erased, I will not be erased, I will stand as a witness against thee, that thou art a very poor writer. (p. 149)

The "slip" apparently is Seymour, whose creation in "A Perfect Day for Bananafish" and his subsequent suicide may well have been an "accident" (the suddenness of the ending and its inexplicable quality the first time one reads the story is some hint that Salinger may have hit on it by "error" or chance). But accident or not, a presence was created who cannot be dispelled. And the ghost of Seymour does haunt Salinger's writing as much as it does the minds of the Glass family survivors. Salinger indicates as much by making details of Buddy's life correspond to his own, thus stressing the complicated relationship between character and author.

Something that should also be kept in mind here is that the idea of the "controlled accident" is important in Zen art. A work of art is regarded as not only representing nature but as being itself a work of nature. Zen paintings, for example, are supposed to be formed as naturally as the hills and trees they depict. This does not mean that art should be left to mere chance and that the artist so forget about control that his work becomes chaos. "The point," stresses Watts, "is rather that for Zen there is no duality, no conflict between the natural element of chance and the human element of control. The constructive powers of the human mind are no more artificial than the formative actions of plants or bees, so that from the standpoint of Zen it is no contradiction to say that artistic technique is discipline in spontaneity and spontaneity in discipline."[19] The whole question thus becomes one for Salinger of whether or not such a concept of Zen art can work as fictional technique.

The quotations from Kafka and Kierkegaard along with the corresponding implications of Zen art do suggest one thing—that the entire story is a fictional treatise on the artistic process. Instead of being concerned with the story itself as a final product, Salinger focuses on the process and the *consequences* of the process of creation. He is writing the story of Buddy as a writer while simultaneously writing his own story as a writer, and the key to both becomes a matter of process, change, and eventual illumination, the *satori* being the artist's own sudden understanding of what his art is, what it can do, and what his relationship to it is. This is what Seymour means when he tells Buddy that writing cannot be a profession; it must be a religion.

But Buddy must struggle with the differences between himself and Seymour, the differences between poetry and fiction. Buddy's writing differs from Seymour's, and his religion must differ also. In speaking through Buddy, Salinger allows a distinction between poetry and fiction much like Edgar Allan Poe's discrimination—the poet is a higher order of moral being.

Buddy cities a Zen story about how a seer is able to choose a horse by seeing through its external qualities to its ideal nature; and this is just what Seymour could do. He could perceive the essential, inward qualities of the spiritual mechanism. But as a fiction writer, Buddy seems incapable of the selflessness necessary to achieve Seymour's vision. The fiction writer must create characters that come out of himself, out of his ego. How, therefore, can he lose his ego without destroying his art? The more he gets involved in his characters, the more he gets involved in himself, and he cannot hope to experience the illumination of the poet who loses himself in the poetic current that runs through things. All Buddy can learn from Seymour, finally, is that the secret or art is to become fully yourself by putting your whole heart into a work. This is not the way of a saint, but it is what the artist can learn from the saint.

Critical reaction to *Raise High the Roof Beam, Carpenters; and Seymour: An Introduction* was, understandably, mixed. Many critics were simply not willing to accept the form or the language of the book. "Hopelessly prolix," Irving Howe objected in the *New York Times Book Review*. "With their cozy parentheses and clumsy footnotes, their careening mixture of Jewish vaudeville humor and Buddhist prescription, they betray a loss of creative discipline, a surrender to cherished mannerisms. And as the world of Salinger comes more fully into view, it seems increasingly open to critical attack. It is hard to believe in Seymour's saintliness, hard even to credit him as a fictional character, for we are barely able to see him at all behind the palpitations of Buddy's memory."[20] John Wain, writing in the *New Republic*, found Salinger's use of Buddy as narrator impossible: "Buddy is a bore. He is prolix, obsessed with his subject, given to rambling confidences, and altogether the last person to be at the helm in an enterprise like this."[21] And in an article in *Twentieth Century Literature*, Paul Levine voiced a widely held objection to Salinger's techniques in his later work: "they blur the distance between the author and his subject matter. This lack of aesthetic distance creates a personal interplay between author and character rather than between character and character. The stories hold the reader's attention not through the revelation of character but through the revelation of author, reducing Salinger's audience to his afficianados and troubled adolescents in general."[22]

But some reviewers were able to assess Salinger's experimentation more appreciatively, and more correctly, although not without some reservations. "The reader should appreciate the artistry in Salinger's deftness of diction, sureness of touch, clearness of tone," J. J. Quinn wrote in *Best Sellers*. "This is particularly important for the latter piece, 'the long, agonizing prose poem,' sounding observations on Life, Character, and the Vocation of the literary artist. The style may get in the way of a reader who mistakes an essay for a short story. The tone may puzzle many. . . . [but] Mature readers will marvel at the brilliant performance that marks the unmistakable Salinger style in presenting his remarkable Glass family."[23] As wild as Buddy's words run, Salinger does show him realizing his atonement at last, even though form must be shattered to do so in making garrulousness a virtue, a necessity, rather than a defect. "My opinion is that Salinger, in clownish guise, has sought to inhibit the profane impulse of language by indulging language prodigally," Ihab Hassan wrote in one of his unusually insightful observations. "The comic battle Salinger wages against language is also the tragic battle man fights with eternity. No one in recent fiction has accepted more difficult terms for that battle than Salinger. It is to our honor that he persists in it with love and grace."[24]

Salinger's battle extends to at least one more story, "Hapworth 16, 1924," which appeared in *The New Yorker*, 19 June 1965, and which shows Salinger still struggling with Seymour's haunting presence. Buddy, now at age forty-six, tries to trace the origins of his older brother's saintliness in a letter Seymour wrote home from Camp Simon Hapworth in Maine when he was seven. In giving us the exact copy of the letter, Buddy provides us with the fullest example we yet have of things as seen from Seymour's point-of-view, and we are thoroughly introduced to the sensitivity and psychic powers that foreshadow his spirituality. We are also exposed to an incredibly precocious mind that soon becomes revolting. Incredibly advanced for his age (or for any age), Seymour writes about how the other boys at camp, and their counselors as well, are slated to go through life with "picayune, stunted attitudes toward everything in the universe and beyond."[25] He mentions that he has developed a "sensual attraction" (at the age of seven, yet) to a Mrs. Happy (it is, as we have seen, his desire for happiness that may be his tragic flaw), the pregnant wife of the camp manager. He tells how Buddy, also at the camp, managed to obtain the use of the mess hall for reading and studying by betting the man in charge, Mr. Nelson, that he can memorize, within a half-hour, a book Mr. Nelson has been reading, *Hardwoods of North America* (Buddy does it). He reflects on the nature of pain: "Half the pain around, unfortunately, quite belongs to somebody else who either shirked it or did not know how to grasp it firmly by the handle."[26] And he asks his parents to send him some books by Tolstoy, Vivekananda of India, Dickens, George Eliot, Thackeray, Austen, Bunyan, and Porter Smith (*Chinese Materia Medica*), among others.

In this story, Salinger attempts to portray Seymour in the process of deepening his awareness. Seymour's special powers and his special weaknesses apparently must be thought of as emanating from some central force underlying all changing manifestations of reality. But the character that emerges is monstrous, fully as hideous in some ways, as the devil-children in such recent movies as *The Omen*. What the story does is to emphazie how oppressive as well as potentially enlightening Seymour's influence on his brothers and sisters must be. He is a grotesque, but then so are the lives of most saints.

"Hapworth," along with Salinger's last two books, marked a long pause that some readers believe may indicate a dead-end for Salinger. Stanley Edgar Hyman's reaction to *Raise High the Roof Beam, Carpenters; and Seymour: An Introduction* is that Salinger has gotten himself into a cul-de-sac: "His highway has turned into a dirt road, then into wagon ruts, finally into a squirrel track and climbed a tree."[27] But Salinger's final phase, to date, certainly indicates more than that. Not only does his treatment of the Glass family and the problem of Seymour as a character give us clues to the imaginative impulse Salinger has struggled with; it may also serve as a dramatization of the creative process itself. Salinger has invented for himself a cloister within which his own consciousness can be isolated, contemplated, and represented, but he has done something else as well: He has created a set of characters who comprise a real family full of love and concern for one another, a family whose story may not be complete (and may never be completed), and a family that presents the same demands on the reader that Faulkner's McCaslin family does—that is, the reader must reconstruct much of the genealogy and family history from scattered allusions. But it is a family whose fictional presence enlarges itself like a spot of oil in the consciousness of the reader as through it we darkly apprehend those sources of insight and substantiality that may enable us to do what Buddy would have us do—come to terms with ourselves and the only world we have.

5

Where He Has Been, Where He Has Gone: Patterns of a Career

When one stands back from Salinger's career, it does take on a curious and disturbing pattern. He begins as a writer of formula fiction fresh out of a course in short-story writing, becomes a member of *The New Yorker* school, achieves a scandalously popular success with *The Catcher in the Rye,* and then gradually loses himself within the potentially brilliant concept of the Glass family. His writing turns more and more inward until it becomes in "Seymour: An Introduction" a commentary on itself, and it becomes difficult to believe that here is a writer who was once a best-selling novelist, his most famous work a Book-of-the-Month-Club selection.

Such a perspective on Salinger's work inevitably leads to John Barth's still-controversial essay, "The Literature of Exhaustion," which appeared in the *Atlantic Monthly* of August, 1967. Although the essay is as much a commentary on the fiction of the Argentine writer Jorge Luis Borges as it is a radical aesthetic statement, Barth suggests that fiction writers should realize that the old conventions of linear plot, omniscient author, and the whole idea that fiction is a representation of reality have led to a "literature of exhausted possibility."[1] The traditional forms of fiction have come to an "intellectual dead end," and the only artistic victory possible is for the writer to turn this against itself by taking up a purifying theme: "the difficulty, perhaps the unnecessity, of writing original works of literature."[2] In this essay, Barth is not so much presenting a prescription for the ills of fiction ("the death of the novel" was an idea very much in the air when the essay appeared) as he is acknowledging a tendency for American writers to become critically self-conscious concerning the creative act and the very validity of fiction itself—a tendency that can be as clearly seen in "Seymour: An Introduction" as it can be in *Giles Goat Boy* or the work of Thomas Pynchon. Salinger, like Barth and Pynchon, comes down at the end to experimenting with radical form that, to use Barth's phrase, is a matter of discovering some way of "throwing out the bath water without for a moment losing the baby."[3]

Whether or not Salinger succeeds at this is difficult to say. "Seymour: An Introduction" contains some memorable surrealistic effects, particularly Buddy's attempt at describing what Seymour looked like by beginning with his hair and moving on to his ears, eyes, and mouth, and winding up with no description at all other than a peculiar example of cubism in fiction. Salinger provides a sometimes bitterly humorous account of Buddy's development as a writer, beginning at the time when he was fourteen and wrote "a story in which all the characters had Heidelberg duelling scars" (p. 115), and continuing through his idea that he is the one being written, not the story: "I'm finished with this. Or, rather, it's finished with me" (p. 247). And, Max F. Schulz is probably right in saying, of *Franny and Zooey* as well as of the last book, that "Unfinished dialogue, telephone conversations, letters, diaries, and bathroom mirror messages are brilliantly manipulated within the linear limitations of the print-bound media to approximate what Marshal McLuhan calls the immediacy and disjunction of the new electronic media and what Salinger would define as the comprehensiveness and simultaneity of the Zen visionary experience."[4] But the same comment might be made on Salinger's most recent fiction that has been made by Jerome Klinkowitz on Barth's *Chimera*, that it "confuses the product of art with the conditions of its inception, a process which . . . often results in simple bad writing, as when the story admits, 'I must compose myself.' "[5]

Salinger's later work should be seen, at any rate, as part of a general development in American fiction that has been going on since World War II when the conservative stability of form that had long dominated American writing was challenged by a growing awareness of the work, not only of Joyce and Kafka (remember that Salinger uses a Kafka quotation as an epigraph at the start of "Seymour: An Introduction"), but also of more exotic talents such as Hesse, Robbe-Grillet, Cortazar, and Borges. It should also be seen as part of a different reaction that involved a certain public distrust of what fiction can do (remember Buddy's near paranoia concerning what the "general reader" thinks of him). Ronald Sukenick has described the reaction this way: "One of the reasons people have lost faith in the novel is that they don't believe it tells the truth anymore, which is another way of saying that they don't believe in the conventions of the novel. They pick up a novel and they know it's make-believe. So, who needs it—go listen to the television news, right? Or read a biography."[6] Salinger thus seems to be expressing some of his own doubts concerning the novel as a medium that gets at the truth of life.

Another important point is that Salinger's development is not unlike that of Kurt Vonnegut and other writers of his generation. He moves steadily away from old-fashioned stories of the sort that lead us to believe that life has leading characters and minor characters, important details and unimportant details, beginnings, middles, ends—"Fundamentally, my mind has always balked at any kind of ending," Buddy confesses at the conclusion of "Seymour: An Introduction." Like Vonnegut by the time he gets to *Breakfast of Champions*, Salinger seems to have resolved to avoid storytelling in favor of a kind of writing that, through its observations on the process by which it was created, and through the conceptualizing frame of the Glass family, shows us one way of combatting the obscenity of modern life and adapting to a chaotic, but ultimately benign, universe.

All phases of Salinger's career must be taken into account in assessing his importance, and few readers would argue with the view that *The Catcher in the Rye* and *Nine Stories* remain Salinger's most satisfying work. In his only novel, he lays claim to a few years that, without much exaggeration, could be called "The Age of Salinger" because of his (sometimes schoolroom-enforced) influence on a generation of readers. With *Nine Stories*, he establishes a reputation as a short-story writer that puts him in the class of Lardner, Fitzgerald, and Hemingway (as well as that of Cheever, Updike, Flannery O'Connor, and James Purdy). And despite his long silence, Salinger's work shows a surprising growth and increasing sophistication of technique. It is a long way from "The Young Folks" to "Seymour: An Introduction." In the process of change, Salinger has become, at points in his performance, a stylist whose comic mastery of language approaches that of Mark Twain, and a writer of considerable religious vision whose books themselves remain in the mind as incarnations of spirit long after they are put down.

Notes

1. THE AMERICAN BRAINSCAPE AND THE DISAPPEARING MAN

1. Albert Fowler, "Alien in the Rye," in *J. D. Salinger and the Critics*, ed. William F. Belcher and James W. Lee (Belmont, Cal.: Wadsworth, 1962), p. 39.
2. J. D. Salinger, *Raise High the Roof Beam, Carpenters; and Seymour: An Introduction* (Boston: Little Brown & Co., 1963).
3. I am, of course, indebted to the famous *Time* article by John Skow, "Sonny: An Introduction," 15 Sept. 1961, pp. 84–90, for much of this biographical information.
4. Skow, in *Salinger: A Critical and Personal Portrait*, ed. Henry Anatole Grunwald (New York: Harper & Row, 1962), p. 11.
5. Skow, p. 13.
6. Kenneth Hamilton, *J. D. Salinger: A Critical Essay* (Grand Rapids, Mich.: Eerdmans, 1967), p. 15.
7. Paul Levine, "J. D. Salinger: The Development of the Misfit Hero," in *J. D. Salinger and the Critics*, p. 107.
8. Arthur Mizener, "The Love Song of J. D. Salinger," in *Salinger: A Critical and Personal Portrait*, p. 25.
9. James E. Miller, Jr., *J. D. Salinger* (Minneapolis: University of Minnesota Press, 1965), p. 6.
10. Mizener, p. 29.
11. Warren G. French, *J. D. Salinger* (New York: Twayne, 1963), p. 55.

155

12. Carlos Baker, *Ernest Hemingway: A Life Story* (New York: Bantam, 1970), p. 533.
13. Skow, p. 13.
14. Baker, p. 889.
15. Baker, p. 889.
16. Leslie Fiedler, "The Eye of Innocence," in *Salinger: A Critical and Personal Portrait*, p. 233.
17. Mizener, p. 23.
18. French, p. 53.
19. French, "The Age of Salinger," in *The Fifties: Fiction, Poetry, Drama*, ed. Warren G. French (De Land, Fla.: Everett/Edwards, 1970), p. 24.
20. Frederick L. Gwynn and Joseph L. Blotner, "The Early Stories," in *Salinger: A Critical and Personal Portrait*, 261.
21. David L. Stevenson, "The Mirror of Crisis," in *Salinger: A Critical and Personal Portrait*, pp. 36–37.
22. Alfred Kazin, "Everybody's Favorite," in *Salinger: A Critical and Personal Portrait*, p. 46.
23. Ernest Haveman, "The Search for the Mysterious J. D. Salinger: The Recluse in the Rye," *Life*, LI, 3 November 1961, p. 137.
24. Haveman, p. 137.
25. Haveman, p. 137.
26. Skow, p. 16.
27. Skow, p. 15.
28. Skow, p. 15.
29. Skow, p. 16.
30. French, *J. D. Salinger*, p. 32.
31. Haveman, p. 142.
32. Joan Didion, "Finally (Fashionably) Spurious," in *Salinger: A Critical and Personal Portrait*, p. 77.
33. David Leitch, "The Salinger Myth," in *Salinger: A Critical and Personal Portrait*, p. 69.
34. Hamilton, p. 7.
35. Hamilton, p. 8.
36. Mizener, p. 30.
37. Levine, p. 112.
38. Donald Barr, "Saints, Pilgrims and Artists," in *Salinger: A Critical and Personal Portrait*, p. 171.

39. Stevenson, p. 39.
40. French, *J. D. Salinger*, p. 41.
41. Ihab Hassan, *Radical Innocence: Studies in the Con-temporary American Novel* (Princeton: Princeton University Press, 1961), p. 264.
42. Levine, p. 115.
43. Lin Yutang, *The Importance of Living* (New York: Capricorn, 1974), p. 1.

2. AGAINST OBSCENITY: *The Catcher in the Rye*

1. J. D. Salinger, *The Catcher in the Rye* (Boston: Little, Brown, 1951). All subsequent page references are to this edition.
2. Dan Wakefield, "The Search for Love," in *Salinger: A Critical and Personal Portrait*, p. 180.
3. Arthur Heiserman and James E. Miller, Jr., "Some Crazy Cliff," in *Salinger: A Critical and Personal Portrait*, p. 197.
4. See *If You Really Want to Know: A Catcher Casebook*, ed. Malcolm M. Marsden (Chicago: Scott, Foresman, 1963) for a collection of articles on the Holden-Huck relationship.
5. Mario D'Avanzo, "Gatsby and Holden Caulfield," *Fitzgerald Newsletter*, Summer 1967, pp. 4–6.
6. Frederick L. Gwynn and Joseph L. Blotner, *The Fiction of J. D. Salinger* (Pittsburgh: University of Pittsburgh Press, 1958), p. 47.
7. Robert G. Jacobs, "J. D. Salinger's *The Catcher in the Rye*: Holden Caulfield's 'Goddam Autobiography,'" *Iowa English Yearbook*, Fall 1959, p. 13.
8. Stekel's best known work in an English translation is probably *Peculiarities of Behavior: Wandering Mania, Dipsomania, Pyromania and Allied Impulsive Acts* (New York, 2 vols., 1924 and 1943).
9. Ihab Hassan, *Radical Innocence: Studies in the Con-temporary American Novel* (Princeton: Princeton University Press, 1961), p. 288.
10. Carl F. Strauch, "Kings in the Back Row," in *If You*

Really Want to Know: A Catcher Casebook, p. 115.

11. Alan W. Watts, *The Way of Zen* (New York: Pantheon, 1957), p. 75.

12. Kenneth Hamilton, *J. D. Salinger: A Critical Essay* (Grand Rapids, Mich: Eerdmans, 1967), p. 39.

13. Jocelyn Brooke, *New Statesman and Nation*, 18 Aug. 1951, p. 42.

14. R. D. Charques, *The Spectator*, 17 August 1951, p. 187.

15. A. L. Goodman, *New Republic*, 16 July 1951, p. 125.

16. Paul Engle, *Chicago Sunday Tribune Magazine of Books*, 15 July 1951, p. 3.

17. Harrison Smith, *Saturday Review*, 14 July 1951, p. 12.

18. Clifton Fadiman, *Book-of-the-Month Club News*, Summer 1951.

19. T. Morris Longstreth, *The Christian Science Monitor*, 19 July 1951, p. 7.

20. Riley Hughes, *Catholic World*, November 1951, p. 15.

21. Virgilia Peterson, *New York Herald Tribune Book Review*, 15 July 1951, p. 3.

22. Edward P. J. Corbett, "Raise High the Barriers, Censors," in *J. D. Salinger and the Critics*, p. 55.

23. Corbett, p. 56.

24. Arthur Heiserman and James E. Miller, Jr., "Some Crazy Cliff," in *Salinger: A Critical and Personal Portrait*, p. 203.

25. Mary McCarthy, "J. D. Salinger's Closed Circuit," *Harper's*, October 1962, p. 46.

26. Donald P. Costello, "The Language of *The Catcher in the Rye*," in *Salinger: A Critical and Personal Portrait*, pp. 266–276. I am indebted to Costello for much of the discussion of Salinger's language that follows.

27. Costello, p. 276.

28. Maxwell Geismar, "The Wise Child and the *New Yorker* School of Fiction," in *If You Really Want to Know: A Catcher Casebook*, p. 44.

29. David Riesman, *The Lonely Crowd: A Study of the*

Changing American Character (New Haven: Yale University Press, 1950), p. 15.

3. ZEN ART AND *Nine Stories*

1. Bernice and Sanford Goldstein, "Some Zen References in Salinger," *Literature East and West*, XV, 1971, 93.
2. Like most Western interpreters of Buddhism, I am indebted to the work of Alan W. Watts (especially *The Way of Zen*), Suzuki, and Walpola Rahala.
3. Heinrich Dumoulin, *History of Zen Buddhism*, cited by Bernice and Sanford Goldstein in "Zen and Nine Stories," *Renascence*, XXII, 1970, p. 172.
4. Dumoulin, p. 172.
5. J. D. Salinger, *Nine Stories* (New York: Bantam, 1964). All subsequent page references are to this edition.
6. William Wiegand, "Seventy-Eight Bananas," in *Salinger: A Critical and Personal Portrait*, p. 125.
7. Kenneth Hamilton, *J. D. Salinger: A Critical Essay* (Grand Rapids, Mich.: Eerdmans, 1967), p. 30.
8. T. S. Eliot, "The Wasteland," in *The American Tradition in Literature*, ed. Sculley Bradley, Richard Croom Beatty, and E. Hudson Long, II (New York: Norton, 1967), p. 1297.
9. Warren G. French, *J. D. Salinger* (New York: Twayne, 1963), p. 41.
10. Josephine Jacobsen, "Beatific Signals," in *Salinger: A Critical and Personal Portrait*, p. 166.
11. Dumoulin, p. 171.
12. Maxwell Geismar, "The Wise Child and the *New Yorker* School of Fiction," in *Salinger: A Critical and Personal Portrait*, p. 93.
13. A pointless critical controversy has developed over the identification of Sergeant X. Wakefield in "Salinger and the Search for Love" (*Salinger: A Critical and Personal Portrait*, pp. 176–191) argues that X is Buddy Glass. Tom Davis in "J. D. Salinger: The

Identity of Sergeant X (*Western Humanities Review*, Spring 1962, p. 16) maintains that X is Seymour. Fred B. Freeman, Jr., thinks that both Wakefield and Davis are wrong and points out that X is not a member of the Glass family and cannot be correctly identified. It seems most logical that the shift in name that occurs in the story is simply a narrative device to underscore the narrator's painful experience at the time.

14. Paul Kirschner, "Salinger and His Society: The Pattern of *Nine Stories*," *Literary Half-Yearly*, XIV, 1963, 74.
15. Kirschner, p. 75.
16. Kirschner, p. 76.
17. Goldsteins, "Zen and *Nine Stories*," p. 181.
18. Seymour Krim, *Commonweal*, 24 April 1953, p. 78.
19. Gene Baro, *New York Herald Tribune Book Review*, 12 April 1953, p. 6.
20. Eudora Welty, *New York Times*, 5 April 1953, p. 4.
21. *U. S. Quarterly Book Review*, June 1953, p. 166.
22. C. X. Larrabee, *San Francisco Chronicle*, 3 May 1953, p. 13.
23. Alan W. Watts, *The Way of Zen* (New York: Pantheon, 1957), p.181.
24. Watts, p. 183.
25. Watts, p. 193.
26. Watts, p. 194.
27. Eugene Herregel, *Zen in the Art of Archery* (New York: Pantheon, 1953), pp. 104–105.

4. A CLOISTER OF REALITY: THE GLASS FAMILY

1. Henry James, "Preface," *Roderick Hudson*, New York Edition of the Novels and Tales of Henry James, I (New York: Scribner's, 24 vols., 1907–17), viii.
2. J. D. Salinger, *Franny and Zooey* (New York: Bantam, 1964). All subsequent page references are to this edition.
3. For a further discussion of this change in Salinger,

see Sam S. Baskett, "The Splendid/Squalid World of J. D. Salinger," *Wisconsin Studies in Contemporary Literature*, Winter 1963, pp. 48–61.

4. Salinger mentions Rilke several times in his fiction, and there are more than a few parallels between the lives of the two writers—both had apparently unhappy experiences in military academies, both seem to have cultivated a sense of isolation, and both make extensive use of female children as beatific figures.

5. Klaus Karlstetter, "J. D. Salinger, R. W. Emerson and the Perennial Philosophy," *Moderna Sprak*, LXIII, 1969, 224–236.

6. Robert Lee Stuart, "The Writer-in-Waiting," *Christian Century*, 19 May 1965, pp. 647–649.

7. Bernice and Sanford Goldstein, "Bunnie and Cobras: Zen Enlightenment in Salinger," *Discourse*, XIII, Winter 1970, 98–106.

8. John Antico, "The Parody of J. D. Salinger: Esmé and the Fat Lady Exposed," *Modern Fiction Studies*, XII, Autumn 1966, 325–340.

9. John Updike, *New York Herald Tribune Book Review*, 17 September 1961, p. 27.

10. Alfred Kazin, *Atlantic*, Aug. 1961, p. 27.

11. *Time*, 15 September 1961, p. 84.

12. S. J. Rowland, *Christian Century*, 6 Oct. 1961, p. 1464.

13. A. E. Mayhew, *Commonweal*, 6 Oct. 1961, p. 48.

14. Granville Hicks, *Saturday Review*, 16 Sept. 1961, p. 26.

15. Irving Howe, *New York Times Book Review*, 7 April 1963, p. 4.

16. Ihab Hassan, "Almost the Voice of Silence: The Later Novelettes of J. D. Salinger," *Wisconsin Studies in Contemporary Literature*, IV, Winter 1963, 5–20.

17. Lyle Glazier, "The Glass Family Saga: Argument and Epiphany," *College English*, XXVII, Dec. 1965, 248–251.

18. Helen Weinberg, *The New Novel in America: The Kafkan Mode in Contemporary Fiction* (Ithaca: Cornell University Press, 1970), p. 147.

19. Alan W. Watts, *The Way of Zen* (New York, Pantheon, 1957), p. 174.
20. Howe, p. 4.
21. John Wain, *New Republic*, 16 Feb. 1963, p. 21.
22. Paul Levine, "J. D. Salinger: The Development of the Misfit Hero," in *J. D. Salinger and His Critics*, p. 114.
23. J. J. Quinn, *Best Sellers*, 1 Feb. 1963, p. 408.
24. Ihab Hassan, *Saturday Review*, 26 Jan. 1963, p. 38.
25. J. D. Salinger, "Hapworth 16, 1924," *The New Yorker*, XLI, 19 June 1965, 34.
26. Salinger, "Hapworth," p. 60.
27. Stanley Edgar Hyman, *Standards*, p. 27, cited by Max F. Schulz in "Epilogue to *Seymour: An Introduction:* Salinger and the Crisis of Consciousness," *Studies in Short Fiction*, V, 1968, 128.

5. Where He Has Been, Where He Has Gone: Patterns of a Career

1. John Barth, "The Literature of Exhaustion," in *The American Novel Since World War II*, ed. Marcus Klein (New York: Fawcett, 1969), p. 267.
2. Barth, p. 272.
3. Barth, p. 273.
4. Max F. Schulz, "Epilogue to *Seymour: An Introduction:* Salinger and the Crisis of Consciousness," *Studies in Short Fiction*, V, 1968, 128.
5. Jerome Klinkowitz, *Literary Disruptions: The Making of a Post-Contemporary American Fiction* (Urbana: University of Illinois Press, 1975), p. 7.
6. Joe David Bellamy, "Imagination as Perception: An Interview with Ronald Sukenick," *Chicago Review*, Winter 1972, p. 60. Reprinted in Joe David Bellamy, *The New Fiction: Interviews with Innovative American Writers* (Urbana: University of Illinois Press, 1974).

Bibliography

WORKS BY J. D. SALINGER

1. Books

The Catcher in the Rye. Boston: Little, Brown and Co.,
    1951.
Nine Stories. Boston: Little, Brown and Co., 1953.
Franny and Zooey. Boston: Little, Brown and Co., 1961.
*Raise High the Roof Beam, Carpenters; and Seymour: An
    Introduction.* Boston: Little, Brown and Co., 1963.

2. Short Stories

"The Young Folks," *Story*, XVI (March–April 1940), 26–
    30.
"Go See Eddie," *University of Kansas City Review* (De-
    cember 1940), pp. 121–124.
"The Hang of It," *Collier's*, CVIII (12 July 1941), 22.
"The Heart of a Broken Story," *Esquire*, XVI (September
    1941) 32, 131–133.
"The Long Debut of Lois Taggett," *Story*, XXI (Septem-
    ber–October 1942), 28–34.
"Personal Notes on an Infantryman," *Collier's*, CX (12
    December 1942), 96.
"The Varioni Brothers," *The Saturday Evening Post*,
    CCXVI (17 July 1943), 12–13, 76–77.
"Both Parties Concerned," *The Saturday Evening Post*,
    CCXVI (26 February 1944), 14, 47–48.

"Soft-Boiled Sergeant," *The Saturday Evening Post*, CCXVI (15 April 1944), 18, 82, 84–85.

"Last Day of the Last Furlough," *The Saturday Evening Post*, CCXVII (15 July 1944), 26–27, 61–62, 64.

"Once a Week Won't Kill You," *Story*, XXV (November–December 1944), 23–27.

"Elaine," *Story*, XXVI (March–April 1945), 38–47.

"A Boy in France," *The Saturday Evening Post*, CCXVII (31 March 1945), 21, 92.

"This Sandwich Has No Mayonnaise," *Esquire*, XXIV (October 1945), 54–56, 147–149.

"The Stranger," *Collier's*, CXVI (1 December 1945), 18, 77.

"I'm Crazy," *Collier's*, CXVI (22 December 1945), 36, 48, 51.

"Slight Rebellion off Madison," *The New Yorker*, XXII (21 December 1946), 76–79.

"A Young Girl in 1941 with No Waist at All," *Mademoiselle*, XXV (May 1947), 222–223, 292–302.

"The Inverted Forest," *Cosmopolitan*, CXXIII (December 1947), 73–80, 85–86, 88, 90, 92, 95–96, 98, 100, 102, 107, 109.

"A Perfect Day for Bananafish," *The New Yorker*, XXIII (31 January 1949), 21–25.

"A Girl I Knew," *Good Housekeeping*, CXXVI (February 1948), 37, 186, 188, 191–196.

"Uncle Wiggily in Connecticut," *The New Yorker*, XXIV (20 March 1948), 30–36.

"Just Before the War with the Eskimos," *The New Yorker*, XXIV (5 June 1948), 37–40, 42, 44, 46.

"Blue Melody," *Cosmopolitan*, CXXV (September 1948), 51, 112–119.

"The Laughing Man," *The New Yorker*, XXV (19 March 1949), 27–32.

"Down at the Dinghy," *Harper's*, CXCVIII (April 1949), 87–91.

"For Esmé—with Love and Squalor," *The New Yorker*, XXVI (8 April 1950), 28–36.

"Pretty Mouth and Green My Eyes," *The New Yorker*, XXVII (14 July 1951), 20–24.

"De Daumier-Smith's Blue Period," *World Review* (London), (May 1952), 33–48.

"Teddy," *The New Yorker*, XXVIII (31 January 1953), 26–36, 38.

"Franny," *The New Yorker*, XXX (29 January 1955), 24–32, 35–43.

"Raise High the Roof Beam, Carpenters," *The New Yorker*, XXXI (19 November 1955), 51–58, 60–116.

"Zooey," *The New Yorker*, XXXIII (4 May 1957), 32–42, 44–139.

"Seymour: An Introduction," *The New Yorker*, XXXV (6 June 1959), 42–52.

"Hapworth 16, 1924," *The New Yorker*, XLI (19 June 1965).

WORKS ABOUT J. D. SALINGER

1.   Bibliographies

Beebe, Maurice, and Jennifer Sperry. "Criticism of J. D. Salinger: A Selected Checklist," *Modern Fiction Studies*, XII (Autumn 1966), 377–390.

Fiene, Donald M. "J. D. Salinger: A Bibliography," *Wisconsin Studies in Contemporary Literature* (Winter 1963), pp. 109–149. Especially useful for its foreign language entries (including translations of Salinger's works and a country-by-country breakdown of foreign criticism) and its section on unpublished Salinger manuscripts.

Davis, Tom. "J. D. Salinger: A Checklist," *Bibliography Society of America. Papers*, LIII (1959), 69–71.

2.   Special Issues of Journals

Wisconsin Studies in Contemporary Literature, IX (Winter 1963).

Modern Fiction Studies, XII (Autumn 1966).

3.   Books

French, Warren. *J. D. Salinger*. New York: Twayne, 1963.

Gwynn, Frederick L. and Joseph L. Blotner. *The Fiction of*

J. D. Salinger. Pittsburgh: University of Pittsburgh Press, 1958.

Hamilton, Kenneth. *J. D. Salinger: A Critical Essay*. Grand Rapids: William B. Eerdmans, 1967.

Miller, James E., Jr. *J. D. Salinger*. Minneapolis: University of Minnesota Press, 1965.

4. Collections of Essays and Casebooks

Belcher, William F. and James W. Lee, eds. *J. D. Salinger and the Critics*. Belmont, California: Wadsworth Publishing Co., 1962.

Grunwald, Henry Anatole, ed. *Salinger: A Critical and Personal Portrait*. New York: Harper, 1962.

Laser, Marvin and Norman Fruman, eds. *Studies in J. D. Salinger: Reviews, Essays, and Critiques of The Catcher in the Rye and Other Fiction*. New York: Odyssey Press, 1963.

Marsden, Malcolm M., ed. *If You Really Want to Know: A Catcher Casebook*. Chicago: Scott, Foresman, 1963.

Simonson, Harold P. and Philip E. Hager, eds. *Salinger's "Catcher in the Rye": Clamor vs. Criticism*. Boston: D.C. Heath, 1963.

5. Critical Articles, Notes, and Commentary

Alcantara-Demalanta, O. "Christian Dimensions in Contemporary Literature," *Unitas*, XLVI (1973), 213–23.

Aldridge, John W. "The Society of Three Novels," *In Search of Heresy: American Literature in an Age of Conformity*. New York: McGraw-Hill, 1956, pp. 126–148.

Allsop, Kenneth. "The Catcher Cult Catches On," *The Daily Mail* (London), 4 January 1958.

Amur, G. S. "Theme, Structure, and Symbol in *The Catcher in the Rye*," *Indian Journal of American Studies*, I (1969), 11–24.

Antico, John. "The Parody of J. D. Salinger's Esmé and

the Fat Lady Exposed," *Modern Fiction Studies*, XII (Autumn 1966), 325–340.

"Are There Any Hemingways in the House? . . . Report on the Young Writers," *Newsweek*, LI (13 January 1958), 90.

Austin, Deborah, Ralph Condee, and Chadwick Hansen. "The Tenth Session: J. D. Salinger: Questions for Study and Discussion," *Modern Fiction: Form and Idea in the Contemporary Novel and Short Story.* University Park, Pennsylvania: Center for Continuing Liberal Education, Pennsylvania State University, 1959, pp. 65–69.

"Backstage with *Esquire*," *Esquire*, XVI (September 1941), 24.

"Backstage with *Esquire*," *Esquire*, XXIV (October 1945), 34.

Balke, Betty T. "Some Judeo-Christian Themes Seen Through the Eyes of J. D. Salinger and Nathanael West," *Cresset* (Valparaiso University), VII (1968), 14–18.

Barr, Donald. "Ah, Buddy: Salinger," *The Creative Present.* Edited by Nona Balakian and Charles Simmons. Garden City, New York: Doubleday, 1963, pp. 27–62.
———. "Saints, Pilgrims and Artists," *The Commonweal*, LXVII (25 October 1957), 88–90.

Baskett, Sam S. "The Splendid/Squalid World of J. D. Salinger," *Wisconsin Studies in Contemporary Literature*, IV (Winter 1963), 48–61.

Baumbach, Jonathan. "The Saint as a Young Man: *The Catcher in the Rye* by J. D. Salinger," *The Landscape of Nightmare: Studies in the Contemporary American Novel.* New York: New York University Press, 1965, pp. 56–67.

Bhaerman, Robert D. "Rebuttal: Holden in the Rye," *College English*, XXIII (March 1962), 508.

"Bid for Salinger," *Observer* (London), 26 November 1961.

Blaney, Shirlie. "An Interview with an Author," *Daily Eagle* (Claremont, New Hampshire), 13 November 1953.

Blotner, Joseph L. "Salinger Now: An Appraisal," *Wisconsin Studies in Contemporary Literature*, IV (Winter 1963), 100–108.

Bonheim, Helmut W. "An Introduction to J. D. Salinger's *The Catcher in the Rye*," *Exercise Exchange* (Bennington College, Vermont), IV (April 1957), 8–11.

"Books of 1951: Some Personal Choices," *The Observer* (London), 30 December 1951, p. 7.

Boothe, Wayne C. "Distance and Point of View: An Essay in Classification." *Essays in Criticism* (Brill, Aylesbury, Bucks, England), XI (January 1961), 60–79.

———. *The Rhetoric of Fiction*. Chicago: University of Chicago Press, 1962, pp. 66, 155, 171, 213, 287.

Bowden, Edwin T. "The Frontier Isolation," *The Dungeon of the Heart: Human Isolation and the American Novel*. New York: Macmillan, 1961, pp. 20–65.

Bowen, Robert O. "The Salinger Syndrome: Charity Against Whom?" *Ramparts*, I (May 1962), 52–60.

Boyle, Robert, S. J. "Teaching 'Dirty Books' in College," *America*, C (13 December 1958), 337–339.

Branch, Edgar. "Mark Twain and J. D. Salinger: A Study in Literary Continuity," *American Quarterly*, IX (Summer 1957), 144–158.

Brandon, Henry. "A Conversation with Edmund Wilson: 'We Don't Know Where We Are,'" *The New Republic*, CXL (30 March 1959), 13–15.

Breslow, Paul. "The Support of the Mysteries: A Look at the Literary Prophets of the Beat Middle Class," *Studies on the Left* (Madison, Wisconsin), I (Fall 1959), 15–28.

Brickell, Herschel. "J. D. Salinger," *Prize Stories of 1949: The O. Henry Awards*, ed. Herschel Brickell. Garden City, New York: Doubleday, 1950, p. 249.

Browne, Robert M. "In Defense of Esmé," *College English*, XXII (May 1961), 584–585.

Bryan, James E. "J. D. Salinger: The Fat Lady and the Chicken Sandwich," *College English*, XXIII (December 1961), 226–229.

———. "The Psychological Structure of *The Catcher in the Rye*," *PMLA*, LXXXIX (1974), 1065–1074.

————. "A Reading of Salinger's 'Teddy.' " *American Literature*, XL (1968), 352–369.

————. "Salinger's Seymour's Suicide," *College English*, XXIV (December 1962), 226–229.

Bufithis, Philip. "J. D. Salinger and the Psychiatrist," *West Virginia University Bulletin: Philological Papers* (21 December 1974), 67–77.

Burnett, Whit and Hallie S. Burnett, "Biographical Notes," *Story: The Fiction of the Forties*. Edited by Whit Burnett and Hallie S. Burnett. New York: E. P. Dutton, 1949, p. 620.

Burrows, David. "Allie and Phoebe: Death and Love in J. D. Salinger's *The Catcher in the Rye*," *Private Dealings: Eight Modern American Writers*. Edited by David J. Burrows et al. Stockholm: Almquist and Wiksell, 1970, pp. 106–14.

Cagle, Charles. "*The Catcher in the Rye* Revisited," *Midwest Quarterly* IV (Summer 1963), 343–351.

Cahill, Robert. "J. D. Salinger's Tin Bell," *Cadence* (Loyola University, Chicago), (Autumn 1959), pp. 20–22.

Carpenter, Frederic I. "The Adolescent in American Fiction," *The English Journal*, XLVI (September 1957), 313–319.

Cecile, Sister Marie, S. S. J. "J. D. Salinger's Circle of Privacy," *The Catholic World*, CXCIV (February 1962), pp. 296–301.

"The Characteristic Form: A Distinct Predilection for the Short Story," *The Times Literary Supplement*, 6 November 1959, p. xv.

Chester, Alfred. "Salinger: How to Love without Love," *Commentary*, XXXV (June 1963), 467–474.

Chugunov, Konstantin. "Soviet Critics on J. D. Salinger's Novel *The Catcher in the Rye*," *Soviet Literature* (Moscow), No. 5 (May 1962), 182–184.

Cohen, Hubert I. " 'A Woeful Agony Which Forced Me to Begin My Tale': *The Catcher in the Rye*," *Modern Fiction Studies*, XII (Autumn 1966), 355–366.

Conrad, Robert C. "Two Novels About Outsiders: The Kinship of J. D. Salinger's *The Catcher in the Rye* with Heinrich Böll's *Ansichten eines Clowns*," *University of Detroit Review*, V (1968–69), 23–27.

"Contributors," *Story*, XVI (March–April 1940), 2.

"Contributors," *Story*, XXI (September–October 1942), 2.

"Contributors," *Story*, XXV (November–December 1944), 1.

"Contributors," *Story*, XXVI (March–April 1945), 4.

Corbett, Edward P. J. "Some Thoughts on *The Catcher in the Rye:* Raise High the Barriers, Censors," *America*, CIV (7 January 1961), 441–443.

Costello, Donald P. "The Language of *The Catcher in the Rye*," *American Speech*, XXXIV (October 1959), 172–181.

————. "Salinger and 'Honest Iago,'" *Renascence*, XVI (Summer 1964), 171–174.

Cowie, Alexander. "J. D. Salinger," *American Writers Today*. Stockholm: Radiojänst, 1956, p. 156.

Cowley, Malcolm. "American Myth, Old and New," *Saturday Review*, XLV (1 September 1962), 6–8, 47.

Cox, James M. "Toward Vernacular Humor," *Virginia Quarterly Review* (Spring 1970), 311–330.

Cunliffe, Marcus. *The Literature of the United States*. Baltimore: Penquin, 1961, pp. 346–347, 364.

D'Avanzo, Mario L. "Gatsby and Holden Caulfield," *Fitzgerald Newsletter* (Summer 1967), pp. 4–6.

Davis, Tom. "J. D. Salinger: 'Some Crazy Cliff' Indeed," *Western Humanities Review*, XIV (Winter 1960), 97–99.

————. "J. D. Salinger: The Identity of Sergeant X," *Western Humanities Review*, XVI (Spring 1962), 181–183.

————. "J. D. Salinger: 'The Sound of One Hand Clapping,'" *Wisconsin Studies in Contemporary Literature*, IV (Winter 1963), 41–47.

Dodge, Stewart. "In Search of 'The Fat Lady,'" *The English Record* (New York State English Council, Geneseo), VIII (Winter 1957), 10–13.

Drake, Robert Y., Jr. "Two Old Juveniles," *The Georgia Review*, XIII (Winter 1959), 443–453.

Ducharme, Edward. "J. D., Sonny, Sunny, and Holden," *English Record*, XIX (1968), 54–58.

"Early Excursions into Glass Country," *The Times Literary Supplement*, 8 April 1960, p. 228.

Elfin, Mel. "The Mysterious J. D. Salinger . . . His Woodsy Secluded Life," *Newsweek*, LV (30 May 1960), 92–94.

Ely, Sister M. Amanda, O. P. "The Adult Image in Three Novels of Adolescent Life," *English Journal*, LVI (November 1967), 1127–1131.

Faulkner, William. "A Word to Young Writers," *Faulkner in the University: Class Conferences at the University of Virginia, 1957–1958*. Edited by Frederick L. Gwynn and Joseph L. Blotner. Charlottesville: The University of Virginia Press, 1959, pp. 241–245.

Feinstein, Herbert. "Contemporary American Fiction: Harvey Swados and Leslie Fiedler," *Wisconsin Studies in Contemporary Literature*, II (Winter 1960–1961), 79–98.

Fenton, Charles. "Lost Years of Twentieth Century American Literature," *The South Atlantic Quarterly*, LIX (September 1960), 332–338.

Fiedler, Leslie A. "The Un-Angry Young Men," *Encounter* (London), X (January 1958), 3–12.

———. "The Invention of the Child," *The New Leader*, XLI (31 March 1958), 22–24.

———. "Good Good Girl and Good Bad Boy," *The New Leader*, XLI (14 April 1958), 22–25.

———. "Boys Will Be Boys," *The New Leader*, XLI (28 April 1958), 23–26.

———. "From Redemption to Initiation," *The New Leader*, XLI (26 May 1958), 20–23.

———. "The Profanation of the Child," *The New Leader*, XLI (23 June 1958), 26–29.

———. *Love and Death in the American Novel*. New York: Criterion, 1960 (see chapters 8 and 9).

Field, W. S. "Herman Hesse as Critic of English and American Literature," *Monatshefte* (University of Wisconsin), LIII (April–May 1961), 147–158.

Fiene, Donald M. "From a Study of Salinger: Controversy

in the *Catcher*," *The Realist* (New York), No. 30 (December 1961), pp. 1, 23–25.

Finkelstein, Sidney. *Existentialism and Alienation in American Literature*. New York: International, 1965, pp. 219–224.

Fleissner, Robert F. "Salinger's Caulfield: A Refraction of Copperfield and His Caul," *Notes on Contemporary Literature*, III (1973), 5–7.

Fogel, Amy. "Where the Ducks Go: *The Catcher in the Rye*," *Ball State Teacher's College Forum*, III (Spring 1962), 75–79.

Foley, Martha. "Salinger, J. D.," *The Best American Short Stories of 1949; and the Yearbook of the American Short Story*. Edited by Martha Foley. Boston: Houghton Mifflin, 1949, p. 319.

Foran, Donald J., S. J. "A Doubletake on Holden Caulfield," *English Journal*, LVII (October 1968), 977–979.

Fowler, Albert. "Alien in the Rye," *Modern Age: A Conservative Review*, I (Fall 1957), 193–197.

Freeman, Fred B., Jr. "Who Was Salinger's Sergeant X?" *American Notes and Queries*, IX (1972), 6.

French, Warren G. "The Phony World and the Nice World," *Wisconsin Studies in Contemporary Literature*, IV (Winter 1963), 21–30.

———. "Holden's Fall," *Modern Fiction Studies*, X (Winter 1964–65), 389.

———. "The Age of Salinger," *The Fifties: Fiction, Poetry, Drama*. Edited by Warren French. De Land, Florida: Everett/Edwards, 1970, pp. 1–39.

———. "Steinbeck and J. D. Salinger," *Steinbeck's Literary Dimensions: A Guide to Comparative Studies*. Metuchen, New Jersey: Scarecrow, 1973, pp. 105–115.

Friedrich, Gerhard. "Perspective in the Teaching of American Literature," *College English*, XX (December 1958), 122–128.

Galloway, David D. *The Absurd Hero in American Fiction: Updike, Styron, Bellow, Salinger*. Revised edition. Austin: University of Texas Press, 1971.

Gehman, Richard. "Introduction," *The Best from Cosmopolitan*. Edited by Richard Gehman. New York: Avon, 1961, pp. xiii–xxvii.

Geismar, Maxwell. "J. D. Salinger: The Wise Child and the *New Yorker* School of Fiction," *American Moderns: From Rebellion to Conformity*. New York: Hill and Wang, 1958.

Giles, Barbara. "The Lonely War of J. D. Salinger," *Mainstream* (New York), XII (February 1959), 2–13.

Glazier, Lyle. "The Glass Family Saga: Argument and Epiphany," *College English*, XXVII (December 1965), 248–251.

Gold, Herbert. "Fiction of the Sixties," *The Atlantic*, CCVI (September 1960), 53–57.

Goldhurst, William. "The Hyphenated Ham Sandwich of Ernest Hemingway and J. D. Salinger: A Study in Literary Continuity," *Fitzgerald/Hemingway Annual* (1970), pp. 136–150.

Goldstein, Bernice, and Sanford Goldstein. "Zen and Salinger," *Modern Fiction Studies*, XII (Autumn 1966), 313–324.

———. " 'Seymour: An Introduction'—Writing as Discovery," *Studies in Short Fiction*, VII (1970), 248–256.

———. "Bunnies and Cobras: Zen Enlightenment in Salinger," *Discourse*, XIII (1970), 98–106.

———. "Zen and *Nine Stories*," *Renascence*, XXII (1970), 171–182.

———. "Some Zen References in Salinger," *Literature East and West*, XV (1971), 83–95.

———. "Ego and 'Hapworth 16, 1924'," *Renascence*, XXIV (1972), 159–167.

———. "Seymour's Poems," *Literature East and West*, XVII (1973), 335–348.

Goodner, R. D. "One of Today's Best Little Writers?" *Cambridge Quarterly* (Winter 1965/66), pp. 81–90.

Green, Martin. "Amis and Salinger: The Latitude of Private Conscience," *Chicago Review*, XI (Winter 1958), 20–25.

———. "Cultural Images in England and America," *A*

Mirror for Anglo-Saxons: A Discovery of America, A Rediscovery of England. New York: Harper, 1960, pp. 69–88.

——. *Re-Appraisals: Some Commonsense Readings of American Literature.* New York: Norton, 1963, pp. 197–229.

Gross, Theodore L. "J. D. Salinger: Suicide and Survival in the Modern World," *South Atlantic Quarterly,* LXVIII (1969), 454–462.

Grunwald, Henry A. "He Touches Something Deep in Us," *Horizon* (New York), IV (May 1962), 100–107.

Gutwillig, Robert. "Everybody's Caught *The Catcher in the Rye,*" *The New York Times Paperback Review Section,* 15 January 1961, pp. 38–39.

Hainsworth, J. D. "Maturity in J. D. Salinger's 'The Catcher in the Rye,'" *English Studies,* XLVIII (October 1967), 426–431.

Hamilton, Kenneth. "Hell in New York: J. D. Salinger's 'Pretty Mouth and Green My Eyes,'" *Dalhousie Review,* XLVII (1967), 394–399.

Hardy, John Edward. "J. D. Salinger: 'Down at the Dinghy,'" *Commentaries on Five Modern American Short Stories.* Frankfurt-am-Main (and Berlin, Bonn): Verlag Moritz Diesterweg, 1962, pp. 7–10.

Harper, Howard M., Jr. *Desperate Faith.* Chapel Hill: University of North Carolina Press, 1967, pp. 66–71.

Hassan, Ihab H. "'Rare Quixotic Gesture': The Fiction of J. D. Salinger," *The Western Review,* XXI (Summer 1957), 261–280.

——. "The Idea of Adolescence in American Fiction," *American Quarterly,* X (Fall 1958), 312–324.

——. "The Victim: Images of Evil in Recent American Fiction," *College English,* XXI (December 1959), 140–146.

——. "The Character of Post-War Fiction in America," *The English Journal,* LI (January 1962), 1–8.

——. "Almost the Voice of Silence: The Later Novelettes of J. D. Salinger," *Wisconsin Studies in Contemporary Literature,* IV (Winter 1963), 5–20.

——. *Radical Innocence: Studies in the Contemporary*

American Novel. New York: Harper & Row, 1961, pp. 259–289.

Howell, John M. "Salinger in the Waste Land," *Modern Fiction Studies*, XII (Autumn 1966), 367–375.

Havemann, Ernest. "The Search for the Mysterious J. D. Salinger: The Recluse in the Rye," *Life*, LI (3 November 1961), 129–144.

Hayes, Ann L. "J. D. Salinger: A Reputation and a Promise," *Lectures on Modern Novelists*. Edited by Arthur T. Broes. Carnegie Series in English, no. 7. Pittsburgh: Department of English, Carnegie Institute of Technology, 1963, pp. 15–24.

Hayman, June. "The White Jew," *Dissent* (New York), VIII (Spring 1961), 191–196.

Hazard, Eloise P. "Eight Fiction Finds," *Saturday Review*, XXXV (16 February 1952), 16–17.

Heiney, Donald W. *Recent American Literature*. Great Neck, New York: Barron's, 1958, pp. 281–284.

Heiserman, Arthur, and James E. Miller, Jr. "J. D. Salinger: Some Crazy Cliff," *Western Humanities Review*, X (Spring 1956), 129–137.

Hermann, John. "J. D. Salinger: Hello, Hello, Hello," *College English*, XXII (January 1961), 262–264.

Hicks, Granville. "J. D. Salinger: Search for Wisdom," *Saturday Review*, XLII (25 July 1959), 13, 30.

Hinckle, Warren. "J. D. Salinger's Glass Menagerie," *Ramparts*, I (May 1962), 48–51.

Howe, Irving. "Mass Society and Post-Modern Fiction," *The Partisan Review*, XXVI (Summer 1959), 420–436.

Hutchens, John K. "On an Author," *The New York Herald Tribune Book Review*, 19 August 1951, p. 2.

Jacobs, Robert G. "J. D. Salinger's *The Catcher in the Rye:* Holden Caulfield's 'Goddam Autobiography,' " *Iowa English Yearbook* (Fall 1959), pp. 9–14.

Jacobsen, Josephine. "Beatific Signals: The Felicity of J. D. Salinger," *The Commonweal*, LXXI (26 February 1960), 589–591.

"J. D. Salinger—Biographical," *Harper's*, CCXVIII (February 1959), 87.

Johannson, Ernest J. "Salinger's Seymour," *The Carolina Quarterly*, VII (Winter 1959), 51–54.

Johnson, James W. "The Adolescent Hero: A Trend in Modern Fiction," *Twentieth Century Literature*, V (April 1959), 3–11.

Kaplan, Charles. "Holden and Huck: The Odysseys of Youth," *College English*, XVIII (November 1956), 76–80.

Karlstetter, Karl. "J. D. Salinger, R. W. Emerson and the Perennial Philosophy," *Moderna Sprak*, LXIII (1969), 224–236.

Kazin, Alfred. "The Alone Generation: A Comment on the Fiction of the 'Fifties,'" *Harper's*, CCIX (October 1959), 127–131.

———. *Contemporaries*. Boston: Little, Brown, 1962, pp. 207–217.

Keating, Edward M. "Salinger: The Murky Mirror," *Ramparts*, I (May 1962), 61–66.

"Keeping Posted: A Thin Slice of College," *The Saturday Evening Post*, CCXVI (15 April 1944), 4.

Kegel, Charles H. "Incommunicability in Salinger's *The Catcher in the Rye*," *Western Humanities Review*, XI (Spring 1957), 188–190.

Kermode, Frank. "Fit Audience," *The Spectator* (London), 30 May 1958, p. 705.

Kim, Chong-Un. "The Novels of J. D. Salinger," *English Language and Literature*, XVIII (June 1960), 107–119.

Kinney, Arthur F. "J. D. Salinger and the Search for Love," *Texas Studies in Literature and Language*, V (Spring 1963), 11–126.

Kirschner, Paul. "Salinger and His Society: The Pattern of *Nine Stories*," *Literary Half-Yearly*, XII (1971), 51–60.

———. "Salinger and His Society: The Pattern of *Nine Stories*," *Literary Half-Yearly*, XIV (1973), 63–78.

Kosner, Edward. "The Private World of J. D. Salinger," *New York Post Week End Magazine*, 30 April 1961, p. 5.

Krassner, Paul. "What Makes Critics Happy?" *The Realist*

(New York), No. 14 (December–January 1959–1960), pp. 5–6.

———. "The Age of Form Letters," *The Realist*, No. 15 (February 1960), p. 6.

———. "An Impolite Interview with Alan Watts," *The Realist* (New York), No. 14 (December 1960), pp. 1, 8–11.

Lane, Gary. "Seymour's Suicide Again: A New Reading of J. D. Salinger's 'A Perfect Day for Bananafish,' " *Studies in Short Fiction*, X (1973), 27–33.

Larner, Jeremy. "Salinger's Audience: An Explanation," *Partisan Review*, XXIX (Fall 1962), 594–598.

Leitch, David. "The Salinger Myth," *Twentieth Century* (London), CLXVIII (November 1960), 428–435.

Lerman, Leo. "It Takes 4," *Mademoiselle*, LIII (October 1961), 108–109.

Leverett, Ernest. "The Virtues of Vulgarity—Russian and American Views," *The Carleton Miscellany*, I (Spring 1960), 29–40.

Levin, Beatrice. "J. D. Salinger in Oklahoma," *Chicago Jewish Forum*, XIX (Spring 1961), 231–233.

———. "Everybody's Favorite: Concepts of Love in the Work of J. D. Salinger," *Motive* (Nashville, Tenn.), XXII (October 1961), 9–11.

Levine, Paul. "J. D. Salinger: The Development of the Misfit Hero," *Twentieth Century Literature*, IV (October 1958), 92–99.

Lewis, R. W. B. "Adam as Hero in the Age of Containment: Epilogue: The Contemporary Situation," *The American Adam: Innocence, Tragedy and Tradition in the Nineteenth Century.* Chicago: University of Chicago Press, 1955, pp. 197–200.

Light, James F. "Salinger's *The Catcher in the Rye*," *Explicator*, XVIII (June 1960), Item 59.

"The Limits of the Possible: Accepting the Reality of the Human Situation," *The Times Literary Supplement*, 6 November 1959, p. xvi.

Lipton, Lawrence. "Disaffiliation and the Art of Poverty," *Chicago Review*, X (Spring 1956), 53–79.

Livingston, James T. "J. D. Salinger: The Artist's Struggle

to Stand on Holy Ground," *Adversity and Grace: Studies in Recent American Literature*. Edited by Nathan A. Scott, Jr. Chicago: University of Chicago Press, 1968, pp. 113–132.

Lodge, David. "Family Romances," *The Times Literary Supplement*, 13 June 1975, p. 642.

Lowrey, Burling. "Salinger and the House of Glass," *The New Republic*, CXLI (26 October 1959), 23–24.

Lorch, Thomas M. "J. D. Salinger: The Artist, the Audience, and the Popular Arts," *South Dakota Review*, IV (1967–68), 3–13.

Ludwig, Jack. *Recent American Novelists*. Minneapolis: University of Minnesota Press, 1962, pp. 28–30, 33–35.

Luedtke, Luther S. "J. D. Salinger and Robert Burns: *The Catcher in the Rye*," *Modern Fiction Studies*, XVI (1970), 198–201.

Lyons, John O. "The Romantic Style of Salinger's 'Seymour: An Introduction,'" *Wisconsin Studies in Contemporary Literature*, IV (Winter 1963), 62–69.

Maclean, Hugh. "Conservatism in Modern American Fiction," *College English*, XV (March 1954), 315–325.

Mailer, Norman. "Evaluations: Quick and Expensive Comments on the Talent in the Room," *Advertisements for Myself*. New York: G. P. Putnam's Sons, 1959, pp. 414–423.

Malin, Irving. *New American Gothic*. Carbondale: Southern Illinois University Press, 1962, pp. 27–35, 59–63, 86–90, 139–143, 158–159.

Marcus, Fred H. "*The Catcher in the Rye*: A Live Circuit," *English Journal*, LII (January 1963), 1–8.

Margolis, John D. "The Place of Love in Society: Salinger's Heroes," *The Haverford News* (Haverford College), LIII (February 9, 1962), 2.

———. "Salinger's *The Catcher in the Rye*," *Explicator*, XXII (November 1963), No. 23.

Marks, Barry A. "Rebuttal: Holden in the Rye," *College English*, XXIII (March 1962), 507.

Martin, Augustine. "A Note on J. D. Salinger," *Studies:*

An Irish Quarterly Review, XLVIII (Fall 1959), 336–345.

Martin, Dexter. "Rebuttal: Holden in the Rye," *College English*, XXIII (March 1962), 507–508.

Martin, Hansford. "The American Problem of Direct Address," *The Western Review*, XVI (Winter 1952), 101–114.

Mathis, Jim. " 'The Catcher in the Rye': Controversy on the Novel in Texas Is Just One in Long List of Episodes," *The Houston Post*, 4 May 1961, Section 7, p. 6.

Matthews, James F. "J. D. Salinger: An Appraisal," *University of Virginia Magazine*, I (Spring 1956), 52–60.

Maxwell, William. "J. D. Salinger," *The Book-of-the-Month Club News* (July 1951), pp. 5–6.

McCarthy, Mary. "Characters in Fiction," *The Partisan Review*, XXVIII (March–April, 1961), 171–191.

————. "J. D. Salinger's Closed Circuit," *Harper's* CCXXV (October 1962), 45–48.

McIntyre, John P., S. J. "A Preface for 'Franny and Zooey,' " *The Critic*, XX (February–March 1962), 25–28.

McNamara, Eugene. "Holden as Novelist," *English Journal*, LIV (March 1965), 166–170.

Meral, Jean. "The Ambiguous Mr. Antolini in Salinger's *The Catcher in the Rye*," *Caliban*, VII (1970), pp. 55–58.

Metcalf, Frank. "The Suicide of Salinger's Seymour Glass," *Studies in Short Fiction*, IX (1972), 243–246.

Milton, John R. "The American Novel: The Search for Home, Tradition and Identity," *Western Humanities Review*, XVI (Spring 1962), 169–180.

Mizener, Arthur. "The Love Song of J. D. Salinger," *Harper's*, CCXVIII (February 1959), 83–90.

————. "The American Hero as Poet: Seymour Glass," *The Sense of Life in the Modern Novel*. Boston: Houghton Mifflin, 1954, pp. 227–246.

"Mlle Passports," *Mademoiselle*, XXV (May 1947), 34.

Moore, Robert P. "The World of Holden," *English Journal*, LIV (March 1965), 159–165.

Noland, Richard W. "The Novel of Personal Formula: J. D. Salinger," *University Review*, XXXIII (October 1966), 19–24.

"The No-Nonsense Kids," *Time*, LXX (18 November 1957), 51–54.

O'Hara, J. D. "No Catcher in the Rye," *The Modern American Novel: Essays in Criticism.* Edited by Max Westbrook. New York: Random House, 1966, pp. 211–220.

Oldsey, Bernard S. "The Movies in the Rye," *College English*, XXIII (December 1961), 209–215.

Orel, Harold. "What They Think About Teen-Agers in Books," *College English*, XXIII (November 1961), 147–149.

Panichas, George A. *The Reverent Discipline: Essays in Literary Criticism and Culture.* Knoxville: University of Tennessee Press, 1974.

Peavy, Charles D. " 'Did You Ever Have a Sister?' Holden, Quentin, and Sexual Innocence," *Florida Quarterly*, I (1968), 82–95.

———. "Holden's Courage Again," *CEA Critic*, XXVIII (October 1965), 1, 6, 9.

"Personal and Otherwise," *Harper's*, CXCVIII (April 1949), 9–10.

Phelps, Robert. "Salinger: A Man of Fierce Privacy," *New York Herald Tribune Books*, 17 September 1961, p. 3.

Pillsbury, Frederick. "Mysterious J. D. Salinger: The Untold Chapter of the Famous Writer's Years as a Valley Forge Cadet," *The Sunday Bulletin Magazine* (Philadelphia), 29 October 1961, pp. 23–24.

Quagliano, Anthony. " 'Hapworth 16, 1924': A Problem in Hagiography," *University of Dayton Review*, XVIII (1971), 35–43.

Ranly, Ernest W. "Journey to the East," *Commonweal*, XCVII (1973), 465–69.

Rees, Richard. "Chaos," *Brave Men: A Study of D. H. Lawrence and Simone Weil.* London: Victor Gollancz, 1958, pp. 153–188.

Reiman, Donald H. "Rebuttal: Holden in the Rye," *College English*, XXIII (March 1962), 507.

————. "Salinger's *The Catcher in the Rye*," *Explicator*, XXI (March 1963), No. 58.

Romanova, Elena. "Reviews and News: What American Novels Do Russians Read?" *Soviet Literature*, No. 7 (July 1961), pp. 178–182.

Roth, Philip. "Writing American Fiction," *Commentary*, XXXI (March 1961), 223–233.

Rovit, Earl H. "Bernard Malamud and the Jewish Literary Tradition," *Critique*, III (Winter–Spring 1960), 3–10.

————. "The Ambiguous Modern Novel," *The Yale Review*, XLIX (Spring 1960), 413–424.

Russell, John. "Salinger, from Daumier to Smith," *Wisconsin Studies in Contemporary Literature*, IV (Winter 1963), 70–87.

Schrader, Allen. "Emerson to Salinger to Parker," *Saturday Review*, XLII (11 April 1959), 52, 58.

Schwartz, Arthur. "For Seymour—with Love and Judgment," *Wisconsin Studies in Contemporary Literature*, IV (Winter 1963), 88–99.

Scott, Nathan. *Modern Literature and the Religious Frontier.* New York: Harper & Bros., 1958, pp. 90–94.

Seitzman, Daniel. "Therapy and Antitherapy in Salinger's 'Zooey,'" *American Imago*, XXV (1968), 140–162.

Seng, Peter J. "The Fallen Idol: The Immature World of Holden Caulfield," *College English*, XXIII (December 1961), 203–209.

Severin–Lounsberry, Barbara. "Holden and Alex: A Clockwork from the Rye?" *Four Quarters* (Summer 1973), pp. 27–38.

Schulz, Max F. "Epilogue to *Seymour: An Introduction*: Salinger and the Crisis of Consciousness," *Studies in Short Fiction*, V (1968), 128–138.

Simms, L. Moody, Jr. "Seymour Glass: The Salingerian Hero as Vulgarian," *Notes on Contemporary Literature*, V (1975), 6–8.

Skow, John. "Sonny: An Introduction," *Time*, LXVIII (15 September 1961), 84–90.

Slabey, Robert M. *"The Catcher in the Rye:* Christian Theme and Symbol," *CLA Journal*, VI (March 1963), 170–183.

Slavitt, David R. "Poetry, Novels and Critics: A Reply," *The Yale Review*, LI (Spring 1962), 502–504.

Slethaug, Gordon E. "Form in Salinger's Shorter Fiction," *Canadian Review of American Studies*, III (1972), 50–59.

––––––. "Seymour: A Clarification," *Renascence*, XXII (1971), 115–28.

Snow, C. P. "Which Side of the Atlantic?" *Harper's*, CCIX (October 1959), 78–87.

Sproul, Kathleen. "The Author," *Saturday Review of Literature*, XXXIV (14 July 1951), 12.

Stein, William B. "Salinger's 'Teddy': *Tat Tvam Asi* of That Thou Art," *Arizona Quarterly*, XXIX (1974), 253–265.

Steiner, George. "The Salinger Industry," *The Nation*, CLXXXIX (14 November 1959), 360–363.

Stevenson, David L. "J. D. Salinger: The Mirror of Crisis," *The Nation*, CLXXXIV (9 March 1957), 215–217.

Stone, Edward. "Salinger's Carrousel," *Modern Fiction Studies*, XIII (Winter 1967–68), 520–523.

––––––. "Naming in Salinger," *Notes on Contemporary Literature*, I (1971), 2–3.

Strauch, Carl F. "Kings in the Back Row: Meaning Through Structure—A Reading of Salinger's *The Catcher in the Rye*," *Wisconsin Studies in Contemporary Literature*, II (Winter 1961), 5–30.

––––––. "Salinger: The Romantic Background," *Wisconsin Studies in Contemporary Literature*, IV (Winter 1963), 31–40.

Stuart, Robert Lee. "The Writer-in-Waiting," *Christian Century* (19 May 1965), 647–49.

Swados, Harvey. "Must Writers be Characters?" *Saturday Review*, XLIII (1 October 1960), 12–14, 58.

Swinton, John. "A Case Study of an 'Academic Bum': Salinger Once Stayed at Ursinus," *The Ursinus Weekly*, LX (12 December 1960), 2, 4.

Tarinaya, M. "Salinger: *The Catcher in the Rye*," *Literary Half-Yearly*, VII (July 1966), 49–60.

Tick, Stanley. "Initiation In and Out: The American Novel

and the American Dream," *The Quadrant* (Sydney, Australia) (1961), 63–74.

Tirumalai, Candadi K. "Salinger's *The Catcher in the Rye*," *Explicator*, XXI (March 1964), No. 56.

Tosta, Michael R. "Will the Real Sergeant X Please Stand Up?" *Western Humanities Review*, XVI (Autumn 1962), 376.

Toynbee, Philip. "Experiment and the Future of the Novel," *The Craft of Letters in England*. Edited by John Lehmann. London: Cresset, 1956, pp. 60–73.

Travis, Mildrid K. "Salinger's *The Catcher in the Rye*," *Explicator*, XXI (December 1962), No. 36.

Trilling, Lionel. *"Lord of the Flies," The Midcentury* (New York), No. 45 (October 1962), pp. 10–12.

Trowbridge, Clinton W. "The Symbolic Structure of *The Catcher in the Rye*," *Sewanee Review*, LXXIV (Summer 1966), 681–693.

———. "Salinger's Symbolic Use of Character and Detail in *The Catcher in the Rye*," *Cimarron Review*, IV (1968), 5–11.

———. "Hamlet and Holden," *English Journal*, LVII (January 1968), 26–29.

Vanderbilt, Kermit. "Symbolic Resolution in *The Catcher in the Rye*: The Cap, the Carrousel, and the American West," *Western Humanities Review*, XVII (Summer 1963), 271–277.

Wakefield, Dan. "Salinger and the Search for Love," *New World Writing, No. 14*. New York: New American Library, 1958, pp. 68–85.

———. "The Heavy Hand of College Humor: Superman, Sex and Salinger," *Mademoiselle*, LV (August 1962), 288–289, 341–343.

Walcutt, Charles Child. "Anatomy of Alienation: J. D. Salinger's *The Catcher in the Rye*," *Man's Changing Mask: Modes and Methods of Characterization in Fiction*. Minneapolis: University of Minnesota Press, 1966.

Walter, Eugene. "A Rainy Afternoon with Truman Capote," *Intro Bulletin* (New York), (December 1957), pp. 1, 2.

Walzer, Michael. "In Place of a Hero," *Dissent* (New York), VII (Spring 1960), 156–167.

Way, Brian. " 'Franny and Zooey' and J. D. Salinger," *New Left Review* (London), No. 15 (May–June 1962), 72–82.

Weales, Gerald. "The Not So Modern Temper," *The Antioch Review*, XVII (December 1957), 510–515.

Weatherby, W. J. "J. D.," *The Guardian* (Manchester), 15 January 1960, p. 8.

———. "Rejection World," *Twentieth Century* (London), CLXXI (Spring 1962), 74–75.

Weigel, John. "Teaching the Modern Novel," *College English*, XXI (December 1959), 172–173.

Wells, Arvin R. "Huck Finn and Holden Caulfield: The Situation of the Hero," *Ohio University Review*, II (1960), 31–42.

West, Ray B., Jr. *The Short Story in America*. Chicago: Henry Regnery Co., 1952, p. 120.

Whittemore, Reed. "But Seriously," *The Carleton Miscellany*, III (Spring 1962), 58–76.

Widmer, Kingsley. "Poetic Naturalism in the Contemporary Novel," *The Partisan Review*, XXVI (Summer 1959), 467–472.

———. "The American Road: The Contemporary Novel," *University of Kansas City Review*, XXVI (June 1960), 309–317.

Wiegand, William. "J. D. Salinger: Seventy-Eight Bananas," *Chicago Review*, XI (Winter 1958), 3–19.

———. "The Knighthood of J. D. Salinger," *The New Republic*, CXLI (19 October 1959), 19–21.

———. "Salinger and Kierkegaard," *Minnesota Review*, V (May–July 1965), 137–156.

Willeford, Charles. "Notes on Beat Writing," *The Chicago Jewish Forum*, XIX (Spring 1961), 234–237.

Williams, Cecil B. "The German Picture of American Literature," *Descant*, V (Fall 1960), 33–37.

Wilson, John F. "The Step Beyond," *Saturday Review*, XLII (15 August 1959), 21.

Workman, Molly F. "*The Catcher* in the Classroom," *Virginia English Bulletin*, X (December 1960), 1–6.

Index